JULIA

THE RADIANCE IN YOUR EYES

WHAT SAVES US FROM NOTHINGNESS?

HAB

ISBN 978-1-941457-15-3

Translation: Sheila Beatty

INTRODUCTION

"What is man that You are mindful of him, and a son of man that You care for him?"[1] How powerful are the words of this psalm today, when we have become more acutely aware of our nothingness, our fragility, and our powerlessness because of a virus that has pushed the whole world's back to the wall! In the grip of fear, or overwhelmed by a lack of meaning, how many of us have discovered a desire for someone to take care of us and save us from the nothingness that looms over us?

"What saves us from nothingness?" This is the question that was to guide the annual Spiritual Exercises of the Fraternity of Communion and Liberation, the most important gesture of the life of the Fraternity. The coronavirus emergency forced us to forego our gathering, which should have taken place in April (as it happened, at the time of full lockdown), but it has not negated this question; rather, in the light of recent events, the question has taken on even greater weight. Sent in advance to all those who were planning to participate in order to encourage attention to their experience and the maturation of a personal contribution, the question was seen as pertinent to the experience of living and as a great gesture of friendship, and it elicited gratitude in those who received it. The raising of this question throws light on the meaning of the word friendship: we are friends so that we can help each

[1] Ps 8:4.

other to not fear questions, even those that grip and disquiet us, wound and shake us. Our being together would not be a friendship if we set these questions like this aside in some way.

If we speak about "nothingness," it is because the existence of contemporary women and men–that is, our personal and social existence–without particular proclamations or special clamor, and yet not without visible effects, appears marked by nihilism in an increasingly clear and forceful way. We are not alluding to a cultural current, but to an existential situation. We want to look at the essential features of this situation, not for the sake of merely analyzing or describing it, but with the passion of those who desire to discover a road that enables the life of each of us to move toward fulfillment in the circumstances given, whatever they may be.

The six chapters of this text delineate an itinerary rooted in an experience and a history, and thus offer a contribution to the search and expectancy of everyone.

CHAPTER 1

NIHILISM AS AN EXISTENTIAL SITUATION

What are the characteristics of the nihilism that has wormed its way into our way of thinking and living whether we recognize it or not, whether we see it explicitly or not?

1. Suspicion about the ultimate substance of reality and about the positive nature of living

On the one hand, the nihilism of which we are speaking presents itself as a suspicion about the ultimate substance of reality: everything ends up in nothingness, ourselves too. "From the vertiginous perception of the ephemeral appearance of things, there develops the temptation, as concession and lying negation, to think that things are illusions and nothingness."[2]

On the other hand, but related to the first, it involves a suspicion about the positive nature of living, the possibility that our life has meaning and is useful; this

---

[2] Luigi Giussani, *L'uomo e il suo destino* [Man and his destiny] (Genova: Marietti *1820*, 1999), 13. [*Editor's Note:* All translations of quotations from works referred to in a language other than English, including this one, are ours].

suspicion normally translates into the perception of an emptiness that threatens everything we do, causing subtle desperation, even in very busy lives full of success, with schedules crammed with appointments and projects for the future.

A well-known film from the 1980s, *The NeverEnding Story*, alludes to this situation evocatively and effectively. Gmork, "the servant of the power behind Nothing," tells Atreyu, the young hero called to stop the Nothing, that "people have given up hoping, and forget their own dreams. As a consequence, Nothing spreads." Atreyu asks, "What is this Nothing?!" and Gmork explains that "it is the void that surrounds us. It is the desperation that destroys the world, and I have acted to help it [...] because it is easier to dominate those who believe in nothing. And this is the surest way to achieve power."[3]

These evocative metaphors and images express something of the attitude that today we identify with the word "nihilism." We can all recognize it: the "nothingness that spreads" in life, the "desperation that destroys," the "void that surrounds us," that becomes a social phenomenon.

Perhaps being forced by the coronavirus pandemic to stop our normal way of living has caused us to reflect in a way that we have not done for a long time on who we are, how we live, what fuels our life, and what consciousness we have of ourselves and of things. As Tolstoy said, "If a man would just stop his activity a moment and reflect, measure the needs of his reason

[3] *The NeverEnding Story* (*Die unendliche Geschichte*), cowritten and directed by Wolfgang Petersen, RFT 1984.

and his heart against the current conditions of existence, he would realize that all his life, all his actions
are in continual and striking contradiction with his
conscience, his reason, and his heart."[4]

This is how a young high school student became
aware of herself as she stopped to reflect. "During the
first week of quarantine, I believe I, like many others,
experienced moments of great dejection. I was terror-
ized by the idea of staying cooped up in my house, not
seeing my friends and my boyfriend and not being able
to go out freely. Then, however, I made a series of calls
that encouraged me; in particular, I had a conversation
with a friend who, when I said, 'I'm OK, but not great,'
wanted to dig deeper. Speaking with him, I realized that
for a long time I had not asked myself questions; I had
just let everything slide by, a bit out of fear, a bit because
I didn't want to reach uncomfortable conclusions. I realize how stupid it is not to ask myself questions if I'm
not happy whether I ask them or not. What makes me
the most anxious is silence because it makes me think;
it puts me in front of my questions. In order to avoid
being overwhelmed and facing myself, often before I go
to sleep I do everything I can to allow my mind to be
invaded by thoughts of every kind until sleep takes over.
I'm worried about the answers to certain questions; I
fear they'll force me to deal with parts of myself I don't
want to know, or will make me undertake a difficult
journey. As my friend said, I prefer to live in a bubble
made up of smiles and laughs, moments of despondency
and sadness, all extremely devitalized and opaque. I live

---

[4] Leo Tolstoy, *Il non agire* [Not to act], in *Il risveglio interiore* [The
interior awakening] (Sassuolo: Incontri Editrice 2010).

in a carnival ride of emotions that take me high one day and dump me into the darkest despondency the next. I feel exalted when I am experiencing those emotions, then set them all aside in my drawer of 'beautiful experiences.' But I realize that this is not enough for me. I want much more. I want something that must necessarily be great because, as Kierkegaard said, 'nothing finite, not even the whole world, can satisfy the human soul that feels the need for the eternal.'"

Late last year, an interview that appeared in *Traces* described nihilism as "a subtle enemy, difficult to grasp and decipher because it does not always exhibit clear features [...], but much more often presents itself intangibly in the form of a bottomless void."[5] Nihilism is at once intangible and very concrete, I would add. A university student articulated it in these terms, "Nothingness, the small daily nothingness that often threatens to dominate my days, is much more subtle and creeping than I had imagined."

Trying to focus as best as we can on the problem, which some may not even see or stubbornly insist on not seeing, we can say that suspicion about the ultimate substance of reality and doubt about the possibility of meaning and fulfillment for our lives intertwine and reciprocally support each other to create the nihilism that touches us all.

Our present-day nihilism can be described as a sense of emptiness outside us (the context we find ourselves

5 Costantino Esposito, "The Nihilism in the House Next Door," interview by Davide Perillo, *Traces* 21, no. 10 (November 2019): 6. Traces is the international monthly magazine of the movement of Communion and Liberation.

living, which can at times be the "bubble made up of smiles and laughs, moments of despondency and sadness, but all extremely devitalized and opaque") and within us, ("I realize that this is not enough for me. I want much more.") whose consequence is a weakening of our relationship with reality, with circumstances, which in the end seem senseless, unworthy of obtaining our true assent. It is a kind of listlesness of the "I" that restrains our involvement with what happens even when we are absorbed in a vortex of frenetic activities–activities that have suddenly and for an indefinite amount of time been interrupted by the coronavirus pandemic, so that to a greater or lesser degree, we have all in some way been forced to think about where we are going, what we want to do with our lives, and what can sustain them effectively.

Perhaps during lockdown this frenetic activity has not so much lessened as changed form and modality. In this way we have discovered, to use the words of C.S. Lewis, "Nothing is very strong: strong enough to steal away a man's best years not in sweet sins but in a *dreary flickering of the mind* over it knows not what and knows not why, in the gratification of curiosities so feeble that the man is only half aware of them."[6] In these times, we are engaged in various attempts to avoid questions that are too troubling, seeking immediate gratification through a merry-go-round of stimuli.

All of this involves torpor, a "dreary flickering of the mind," and, as Orwell observed in his prophetic novel, *1984*, apathy. "It struck him that the truly character-

[6] C.S. Lewis, *Screwtape Letters: Letters from a Senior to a Junior Devil* (London: Collins, 2012). Italics ours.

istic thing about modern life was not its cruelty and insecurity, but simply its bareness, its dinginess, its dull listlessness."[7] This listlessness is what corrodes the intimate depths of the "I" and digs a ditch between us and what is happening. "There was nothing in my surroundings which I could respect and which attracted me," wrote Dostoyevsky.[8]

Thus nothing seems able to truly engage the "I." Our relationships and the things we do bore us, even those that once excited us.

This is the face that nihilism wears today: asthenia, an absence of striving and energy, a loss of the gusto in living, intimately linked to the absence of something that truly seizes us. "Don't talk to me about your prosperity, your riches, the rarity of famine, the rapidity of the means of transport! There is more of riches, but less of force. The idea uniting heart and soul to heart and soul exists no more. All is loose, soft, limp—we are all of us limp."[9]

2. The loss of a meaning to the expectancy to life

In a poem written when he was just seventeen, Cesare Pavese expressed his heartrending pain at the loss of meaning commensurate to the expectancy of human life: "Going along the solitary roads / tormented con-

[7] George Orwell, *1984*, in *The Complete Novels of George Orwell* (London: Penguin, 2001). Ebook.

[8] Fyodor Dostoevsky, *Notes from the Underground*, trans. Constance Garnett (Indianapolis: Hackett Publishing Company, 2009), 37.

[9] Fyodor Dostoevsky, *The Idiot*, trans. Constance Garnett (New York: Bantam Classics, 1983), 171.

tinually by the terror / of seeing the creations long yearned for / vanish in front of my eyes; / to feel weakening within my soul / ardor, hope … everything … everything / and to remain thus without a love, / […] damned to daily sadness."[10]

Some months ago a young university student wrote me, "In this recent period, as never before, I have realized that I live moments of nothingness, moments in which the horizon of my life is characterized by a decline of desire, and I disappear, I live halfway. The nothingness inside me speaks delicately, inducing me to spare myself, to spare my energy because it is only worthwhile to do what I have in mind, without even considering other proposals, and to spare myself in relationships because it is not worthwhile to share my difficulties. It induces me to expend the least effort possible, and I find myself feeling increasingly arid and discontented. In these last days of November, it seems I'm living in a sepulchral atmosphere: in front of many beautiful opportunities, from unexpected relationships with freshmen to the graduations of my older friends, I often find myself closed in on my thoughts and difficulties. I realize that I am at the mercy of nothingness, of a discomfort that I can't explain."

This same experience is alluded to in another letter I recently received: "Staying at home without work [because of the isolation imposed by the healthcare emergency] I've begun to experience firsthand this nothingness that you talk about. If this time is not filled with something that lasts, it is completely empty and I am nothing."

[10] Cesare Pavese, "A Mario Sturani," Monza–Turin, Jan. 13, 1926.

But this is not all. In fact, in addition to the characteristics indicated, there is also a sensation of powerlessness to change the aspect of our character we have taken on (it presents "intangibly in the form of a bottomless void," as was described above) or to get up again; it seems as if our efforts and certain stimuli that reach us from outside are insufficient to get us back on our feet, to make us perceive the heft of reality, and to redeem us from the emptiness we feel.

This painful experience is shared by many of our contemporaries. "The fact is that nothing can halt the ever-increasing recurrence of those moments when your total isolation, the sensation of an all-consuming emptiness, the foreboding that your existence is nearing a painful and definitive end all combine to plunge you into a state of real suffering."[11] For this reason, Pope Francis holds that "today's serious threat […] is the loss of the meaning of life."[12]

We need something able to reawaken all of our being and to reopen us to the provocation of reality, of circumstances, so that we can "live always the real intensely."[13] We realize that the simple happening of things does not suffice. We find ourselves in the situation of trying to climb up a slippery slope and sliding back down again, returning to the point of departure. We fall back into our nothingness. We do not see what can counter it and we do not understand where to start from. Therefore we are profoundly uneasy with ourselves.

11 Michel Houellebecq, *Whatever*, trans. Paul Hammond (London: Serpent's Tail, 1994), 11.
12 Francis, *General Audience*, November 27, 2019.
13 Luigi Giussani, *The Religious Sense* (Montreal: McGill-Queen's University Press, 1997), 108.

This is the discomfort that the psychoanalyst Galimberti has identified in young people (though it extends to everyone): "Young people today are not well, but they don't even understand why."[14]

"Hearing that line by Galimberti" a young friend wrote me, "tore up my heart because it describes my life in this period to a T. For months now, I've been feeling a sort of dissatisfaction and sadness in everything I do. I see that this dissatisfaction is everywhere and that under the mask of smiles and thousands of things to do, there is a dominion of nothingness, an absence of true meaning, an absence of true gladness. Lacking meaning, there remains only duty, a useless focus on duty that drags me further down toward the bottom. Maybe this is the nihilism of which you speak often. It is a problem that concerns my existence. In fact, life now is less life. The first proof of this is that everything that does not go according to my plans is like a millstone dragging me down. It only takes a little thing that does not go as I wanted and I collapse, give up, and let myself go. In front of reality I am resigned and sad. In spite of the masks, the efforts to pretend that there's no problem, pushing myself to go forward, I realize that deep down, in front of all the things that happen to me and that I see, I'm sad, but I don't understand why. Just a few years ago it was the opposite—difficulties were like trampolines, not burdens. Now I try not to look at the need in my heart; I pretend it's

[14] Umberto Galimberti, "A 18 anni via da casa: ci vuole un servizio civile di 12 mesi" [Out of the house at 18: What's needed is 12 months of civil service], interview by S. Lorenzetto, *Corriere della Sera*, September 15, 2019.

not there, that I'm fine. Nothing amazes me anymore. I need something great that can overcome the nothingness into which I've fallen. I need to understand what happens to me during my days because I don't want to remain in this nothingness."

We let ourselves go, focusing on banal things, without expectations, in order to fill in some way passing time. "You don't choose nothingness: you abandon yourself to nothingness,"[15] because, as Malraux said, "there is no ideal for which we can sacrifice ourselves," one for which we can truly engage ourselves, "because we all know deceit, we who do not know what truth is."[16]

As you can see, the present-day nihilism is not the same as the earlier one, which heroically inveighed against values–today's nihilism is not ambitious. It has the face of a "normal" life, but with a worm inside; nothing seems worthwhile, nothing attracts or truly seizes us. This nihilism is lived passively; it penetrates under your skin and leads to a tiring of desire, like a marathon runner who is exhausted after just having started the race. Augusto Del Noce spoke of a "gay nihilism, without inquietude," that drowns Saint Augustine's "*inquietum cor meum*" in superficial pleasures.[17]

---

[15] Cornelio Fabro, *Libro dell'esistenza e della libertà vagabonda* [Book of existence and of vagabond freedom] (Casale Monferrato (AL): Piemme, 2000), 28.

[16] André Malraux, *La tentation de l'Occident* (Paris: Bernard Grasset), 216.

[17] Augusto Del Noce, "Lettera a Rodolfo Quadrelli" [Letter to Rodolfo Quadrelli], unpublished, 1984. "Today's current nihilism is a gay nihilism, without inquietude (perhaps it could be defined by the suppression of Augustine's *inquietum cor meum*)."

3. Freedom facing a challenge

In this context, our freedom faces a challenge. Let's ask ourselves: Can we limit ourselves to detachedly observing the spectacle of nothingness advancing in our life, as Houellebecq wrote? "Stationed at the crossing of space and time, / I coldly observe the advance of nothingness."[18]

Freedom can also decide not to see, and to flee: "OK, we're at the mercy of nothingness. *Pfff*, who cares!" fooling ourselves that we resolve the problem by simply shifting our gaze elsewhere. Edgar Morin, one of the most well-known living European thinkers, acutely observed, "I have understood that concealing facts that disturb us, anesthetizing and eliminating them from our mind, is a source of errors and illusions."[19] It is like removing a tooth to eliminate the pain, or putting an idea "out of sight, out of mind." We have tried to do this in the time of coronavirus. If Job were alive in our era, his friend Zophar would have consoled him by saying, "In moments of isolation, you have to distract yourself! There's no better pain-killer than pleasure!"

But is this true? Can we truly succeed in following the intent of Del Noce's gay nihilism; that is, suppressing the heart's inquietude, or, as Morin says, eliminating from our mind the advance of nothingness? Look at your own experience and judge. Can we truly solve the problem in this way, just by turning away from it?

---

[18] Michel Houellebecq, *Cahier* (Milan: La nave di Teseo, 2019), 23.
[19] Edgar Morin, *Insegnare a vivere: Manifesto per cambiare l'educazione* [Teaching to live: A manifesto for changing education] (Milan: Raffaello Cortina, 2015), 14.

There are those like Andrea Momoitio who have the sincerity to confess that this road is untenable. "Are you having a tough day? Don't worry, I'll send you one of those stupid one-liners that keep on circulating on WhatsApp, even if I don't really find them funny at all, even if I feel like a cynic who's trying to force a smile from others while all I want to do is watch *Hospital Central* [*editor's note*: a TV series]. I make videos with my colleague Andrea Liba. I think of silly gif images to post on Instagram and then I collapse because I don't believe in anything. I need to know that my world is here, but it isn't so. […] I have nothing more to say, except that I'm desperate, and find it hard to understand so much festivity in the atmosphere and so much optimism, so many Zoom invitations, so many text messages, so much applause and so many idiocies. […] I have no choice but to learn to live with this anger that invades me and for which I don't know whom to blame."[20] In an equally sincere way, Sol Aguirre confesses having developed a recipe for coping with the situation whose inconsistency she herself admitted: "So here I am, talking rubbish […] to see if by chance something I say brings a smile to a grouchy face. Once again, laughter as the antidote to a reality that is too dark. A laugh, often so disdained, is always my remedy."[21]

The fact, as Simone Weil wrote, is that "nobody […] settles purely and simply for living […]. We want to live for something."[22] Once again, Dostoyevsky cautioned,

[20] Andrea Momoitio, *Público*, April 10, 2020.
[21] Sol Aguirre, *El Español*, April 3, 2020.
[22] Simone Weil, *L'amore di Dio* [The love of God] (Rome: Borla, 1979), 78.

"You can err in ideas, but it is impossible to err with the heart or lose your own conscience by mistake."[23]

If it is impossible to err with the heart, what does this mean?

We can decide to ignore the problem of our malaise, of the nothingness that corrodes our days, by trying to eliminate it. But–surprise, surprise–the pain remains. And how! The heart's inquietude can be covered over but not suppressed; the dissatisfaction can be hidden but not eliminated. In the final analysis, there is something in us that cannot be silenced. In spite of the masks we wear and our efforts to pretend that nothing is wrong, forcing ourselves to move forward, we are sad and everything is like a millstone that crushes us. "Out of sight, out of mind" just doesn't work! The pain remains. There is something inside us that holds out, that lasts. "Something was not dead within me, in the depths of my heart and conscience it would not die, and it showed itself in acute depression."[24]

What holds out and lasts? Houellebecq described it in his letter to Bernard-Henri Lévy, which I have quoted many times because I think it provides an excellent example of the human dynamic we are describing: "More and more frequently, and it pains me to admit it, I felt *a desire to be liked*. On each occasion a little thought convinced me of the absurdity of this dream […]. But thought was powerless and the desire persisted–and, I have to admit, persists to this day."[25]

[23] Fyodor Dostoevsky, *Lettere sulla creatività* [Letters on creativity] (Milan: Feltrinelli, 1991), 55.
[24] Dostoevsky, *Notes from the Underground*.
[25] Michel Houellebecq, quoted in "The 'Unbalanced' Power of Christianity," *L'Osservatore Romano*, June 4, 2019.

So then, let's not fool ourselves or let others take us for a ride by saying that we solve the problem just by looking elsewhere. First and foremost, nihilism finds a point of resistance within ourselves. Let's pay attention to it.

Isabel Coixet had to admit her powerlessness in front of the challenge of the coronavirus pandemic: "Everything we took for granted is gone. Opening before us is a dense fog, lacking light. I acknowledge that I don't know how to live this hour, these minutes that are becoming eternal."[26] The Spanish director recognizes that she does not know how to face what is happening to her and to us, and this provokes a malaise that transforms the passing minutes into a seemingly endless nightmare. Sol Aguirre described her experience of isolation in these words, "During the first week of lockdown I was afraid, not just about the virus, but also about the possibility that sadness would come upon me. I refer to the unbearable and long-lasting sadness that blurs your sight and your life. I never confessed this to anyone because I knew what they would say: be happy, do projects, find solutions."[27]

4. The ineradicable nature of desire

What emerges from these reactions, these sincere and open confessions? The continuing existence of the original structure of the human "I," the locus of our

---

[26] Isabel Coixet, *ABC*, March 31, 2020.
[27] Sol Aguirre, *El Español*, April 10, 2020.

desire to reach fulfillment, to love and be loved, and to know the full meaning of oneself and of reality. It is stunning to see this in someone like Houellebecq. We have no power over the direction of our desire, the striving that marks our innermost depths. Augustine gave voice to it in his unforgettable way, "*Fecisti nos ad te et inquietum est cor nostrum donec requiescat in te.*"[28] This irreducible nature of the heart, perhaps under other names, announces itself precisely at the bottom of nihilism, which today has become a cultural way of being and a social phenomenon.

So what is the first step for those who do not want to live their lives fleeing from a problem they do not know how to solve? In this context of a lack of meaning, you have to recognize that there is something irreducible and ineradicable that holds out against nihilism and rationalist cynicism. What holds out and endures? My "I," which is irreducible.

If I pay close attention, I have to acknowledge the persistence of the elementary structure of my "I" even though I am influenced by the lack of meaning that surrounds me; that is, the "climate," the culture. The more nothingness spreads, the more the wounds and expectations of our humanity emerge in all their power, no longer covered over by the cultural dialectics and collective projects that no longer have a grip on us. These wounds and expectations emerge in their most elementary form without the armor of too many discourses. "Something was not dead within me, in the depths of my heart and conscience it would not

---

[28] Saint Augustine, *Confessions* I, 1. "You have made us for Yourself, O Lord, and our heart is restless until it rests in You."

die," said Dostoyevsky. And Chesterton noted, "When you're really shipwrecked, you do really find what you want."[29]

We have seen this in a surprising way with the explosion of the coronavirus pandemic. Woken from our torpor, we began to see our questions emerge again. As the Italian writer and journalist Maurizio Maggiani said in an interview for *Traces*, "We were living in a time without a future, in which nothing else could happen. Everything had its logic that could not be challenged. The system could not be broken. [...] Suddenly an earthquake sent a shockwave through this tranquil plain and created in its place a challenging landscape." What was the first outcome of this earthquake? Questions. "It is necessary that we ask ourselves questions that can free us from tight spaces, from the walls that imprison us. [...] In our struggles, our chaos, we can lead ourselves to the use of reason, to become adults. How? By asking questions."[30] Maggiani notes that in front of questions, all the arrogance and pride that so often accompany us die down.

Challenged by a vertiginous circumstance, we have found that our questions have opened a breach in the comfort zone where we had taken refuge. The bubble has popped. "We have lived too long under anesthesia," said Nuria Labari, "being part of a system too often mistaken in its foundations."[31] We have experienced what Fr. Giussani affirmed in the tenth chapter

---

[29] G.K. Chesterton, *Manalive* (Thomas Nelson and Sons, 1912), available at http://www.gutenberg.org/files/1718/1718-h/1718-h.htm.

[30] Maurizio Maggiani, "Life Changes," interview by Alessandra Stoppa, *Traces* 22, no. 5 (May 2020): 9.

[31] Nuria Labari, *El País*, March 18, 2020.

of *The Religious Sense*: "If an individual were to barely live the impact with reality, because, for example, he had not had to struggle, he would scarcely possess a sense of his own consciousness, would be less aware of his reason's energy and vibration."[32]

There are moments when reality crashes into us so powerfully that it is very difficult to soften the impact, to elude or ignore its provocation. What has happened has, with the involvement of our freedom, reawakened our attention, setting our reason into motion, freeing us to ask questions about meaning that express its nature. I am talking about the urgent need for meaning that constitutes us and that an impact with stark reality, which we have accepted, has brought to light in a powerful way. In this sense, we have spoken of a "reawakening of the human."[33]

5. A cry that implies an answer

The more nihilism advances, the more it becomes unbearable to live without meaning and the more our indestructible desire to be cherished and loved makes itself known.

This is what happened to the prodigal son in the Gospel of Luke:[34] the lower he sank, the more his longing for his father surprisingly emerged. But even those who think they have no father realize that the desire to

[32] Giussani, *The Religious Sense*, 100.
[33] Julián Carrón, *Reawakening our Humanity: Reflections in a Dizzying Time*, ed. Alberto Savorana (Fraternity of Communion and Liberation, 2020). Ebook.
[34] Lk 15:11–32.

be loved persists and is irreducible, as was document-ed in Houellebecq's letter to Bernard-Henri Lévy. This desire does not lessen and is not quenched. "Our time is diffident about words and avoids dogmas. Even so, it knows the meaning of desire. It desires confusedly, without knowing what, if not the sensation of having inside an emptiness that needs to be filled."[35] In this regard, Chekhov observed that in order to grasp the person in front of you, you must look at his desire: "When I have wanted to understand somebody or myself, I have considered, not the actions [as we are often tempted to do, above all with ourselves: with moralistic fierceness we easily focus on our mistakes and then beat ourselves up for them], in which everything is relative, but the desires."[36] This is what Jesus does. What does He see in the Samaritan woman at the well? Her desire. He speaks to the thirst of that woman, "I have water, new water, different, the only water that can satisfy your thirst."[37] In this sense, Chekhov declared, "Tell me what you want, and I will tell you what manner of man you are."[38]

Our desire, everything we authentically and profoundly want, identifies the ultimate face of our "I." Giussani said, "I believe that my continual reference to desire, which comes to me from my life experience [...] is one of the things that makes what I say more

---

[35] Erik Varden, *La solitudine spezzata* [Broken solitude] (Magnano (Bi): Qiqajon–Comunità di Bose, 2019).
[36] Anton Chekhov, "A Dreary Story," excerpts available at <u>https://americanliterature.com/author/anton-chekhov/book/a-dreary-story/chapter-6.</u>
[37] Cf. Jn 4:4–42.
[38] Chekhov, "A Dreary Story."

engaging [more interesting], because it is something evidently human, but it is the thing least perceived by everyone."[39] In fact, many would like to suffocate it, to look elsewhere, to tread it underfoot.

How should we live this situation? What is the starting point for regaining the life we risk losing? These questions express an existential need; they are like a thorn in the flesh. Desire is irreducible and it holds on notwithstanding the spread of nothingness; it makes life dramatic and causes the questions to burn even more. For this reason, we are in front of an alternative: either we resign ourselves and look elsewhere, pretending that there is no problem and fooling ourselves, or we follow the urgent need of our heart that nobody can extinguish, and we allow our desire to cry out. We can acknowledge reality, beginning with our unease, and cry out our thirst for full meaning, for total satisfaction.

But, if in the end there is only nothingness, is it reasonable to cry out? At times we are discouraged and tired of crying out. At other times we doubt the value of crying out. The reason for this discouragement and doubt is that we take for granted the existence of the cry of the heart, of that desire that holds out against all forms of nihilism. But the cry, the entreaty, and desire are the least predictable things in the world. In fact, if we reflect on it, we begin to marvel at their existence. So, what does the existence of the cry mean for us?

[39] Fraternity of Communion and Liberation, Audiovisual Documentation, *Day of Meditation for Married People*, Milan, January 23, 1977.

If there is a cry, there is an answer. We often find it difficult to understand and accept such a statement because we take the cry for granted. Using reason fully, being faithful to what emerges in experience, Giussani identified a permanent law: "The idea that the very existence of the question implies the existence of an answer."[40] Mysterious as it may be, the answer exists. It is implicit in the question. (In this sense, in the interview quoted above, Maggiani observed that the answer "is already in the question."[41]) In fact, Giussani went on, "one suppresses the question if one does not admit to the existence of an answer."[42]

The "I" of each of us "is hunger, thirst, and passion for an ultimate object, which looms over the horizon, and yet always lies beyond it."[43] The question about and the entreaty for meaning, love, and fulfillment are the implicit affirmation of "an ultimate answer which lies *beyond* the experiential aspects of existence," but that exists. Why do I know it exists? Because, I repeat, its existence is implicit in the very dynamism of my person, in the structure of my humanity as need. "If the hypothesis of a 'beyond' were to be eliminated, those needs would be unnaturally suffocated."[44]

The entreaty for exhaustive meaning, for total explanation, constitutes and is the supreme expression of our reason. Its very presence forces us to affirm the existence of an answer, even though it is beyond the horizon of what we can measure. "This explanation

40 Giussani, *The Religious Sense*, 58.
41 Maggiani, "Life Changes," 9.
42 Giussani, *The Religious Sense*, 57.
43 Ibid., 51.
44 Ibid., 115.

[reason, the "I"] cannot be found within the horizon of life's experience […]. If reason is to be rescued, that is to say, if we want to be coherent with this energy that defines us, if we do not want to deny it, then its very dynamism forces us to affirm the exhaustive answer *beyond* the horizon of our life."[45] It does not coincide with anything that I can grasp. I do not know what it is, but I know that it exists. Otherwise the cry would not exist; we would not be able to explain the existence of the question, the entreaty.

When we abolish the category of possibility, which is the very stuff of reason, when out of difficulty in affirming the answer we say, "It's not possible," we deny reason in its very essence and squash its vital dynamism. If I were lost in a forest, the most reasonable gesture would be to cry out for help. But the cry implies the possibility that there is someone to hear me. Even if there is only the remotest possibility, I can never exclude *absolutely* that someone may hear me. Otherwise it would be absurd to yell for help.

In this sense, not admitting the existence of an answer would mean denying the question, which, however, exists. It would mean denying the drive of reason, betraying the striving of desire. This "irrationality," this "desperation,"[46] is what strongly tempts contemporary women and men, each of us, because of the difficulties we find along our way.

---

[45] Ibid., 116. Giussani continues, "The summit of reason's conquest is the perception of an unknown unreachable presence, to which all human movement is destined, because it depends upon it. It is the idea of *mystery*." Ibid., 117.
[46] Ibid., 72–73.

6. A "You" who hears our cry

The cry, as the expression of reason's urgent need for meaning, of the heart's desire for fulfillment, belongs to the nature of the human being. It can be attenuated, weakened, and countered, but not uprooted, neither by the person himself nor by others. It is not in our power to do so. It is "the chief sign of the grandeur and nobility of human nature," as Leopardi wrote.[47] Certainly, in various ways we are tempted not to take it into consideration and often feel how difficult it is to open ourselves and keep faithful to its important indications. In certain moments of the lockdown, as many have testified, we felt it emerge more clearly and inexorably. In other moments, it is like a hunger that dies down because of the difficulty of getting the food that satisfies it, or like a search you lose enthusiasm for because you see no clues for what you are seeking.

In fact, when does the entreaty rekindle and become a flame? When in front of ourselves we find a presence that responds, a presence that lives up to our entreaty for totality. It should not be difficult to imagine how forcefully and uncontrollably the blind man Bartimaeus cried out when he heard that someone was approaching who people said responded to the deep plea for life expressed by all people.

"As He was leaving Jericho with His disciples and a sizeable crowd, Bartimaeus, a blind man, the son of Timaeus, sat by the roadside begging. On hearing that it was Jesus of Nazareth, he began to cry out [you cry

[47] Giacomo Leopardi, *Pensieri* LXVIII, trans. W.S. Di Piero (Baton Rouge: Louisiana State University Press, 1981), 113.

out in response to someone. Many people must have walked past Bartimaeus, but only when he heard people talking about that man, a fellow with a first name and last name, did he begin to cry out:] […] 'Jesus, son of David, have pity on me.' And many rebuked him, telling him to be silent. But he kept calling out all the more, 'Son of David, have pity on me.' Jesus stopped and said, 'Call him.' So they called the blind man, saying to him, 'Take courage; get up, He is calling you.' He threw aside his cloak, sprang up, and came to Jesus. Jesus said to him in reply, 'What do you want Me to do for you?'"[48]

Since then, since Jesus burst into history, the horizon of the lives of women and men has a presence it can cry out to, someone who responds to our cry and asks, "What do you want Me to do for you?" There is one who embraces our cry, a presence that no one can erase, a fact that happened and happens, contemporary, remaining and continuing in history. The possibility of encountering Him is given to each of us. No matter what your situation, the aridity or weariness you feel, the inability to be seized by things, or the nothingness that assails you, no matter what position you take, you cannot avoid being reached by Christ's question, hearing it resonate and rebound as if it were addressed personally to you: "What do you want Me to do for you?" And nothing can keep you from answering like the blind Bartimaeus: "Master, I want to see."[49] I want to experience an attraction to You that draws me out of nothingness.

[48] Mk 10:46–51.
[49] Mk 10:51.

The Christian companionship is comprised by those who, like Bartimaeus, have perceived and embraced this presence capable of hearing the cry of their humanity, reawakening an ultimate, irreducible love for themselves, an otherwise unthinkable tenderness for themselves, sustaining their journey, keeping them from slipping off into nothingness.

CHAPTER 2

"HOW CAN THIS ABYSS OF LIFE BE FILLED?"

The central question we have asked ourselves is fundamental: "What saves us from nothingness?" In the inevitable drama of life, how can we keep from succumbing to our vulnerability and powerlessness? What can respond to the void of meaning? As the coronavirus pandemic has shaken each of us and made us fear for our lives, we feel the question even more acutely, and this helps us be more clear-sighted as we weigh our attempts at an answer.

1. Insufficient attempts

a) Reasonings that no longer convince anyone

Some think that a mere *discourse* can meet the challenge of the advance of nothingness, but as our experience shows, this does not suffice. A line of thought, a philosophy, a psychological or intellectual analysis does not enable the human to start afresh, does not give new breath to desire, does not regenerate the "I." Libraries are full of them and with the internet everything is at hand but the nothingness spreads unabated. The more you pay attention to what stirs in the depths of your heart, the more you realize how insufficient they are. "Something is meant by human being which involves more than just being; something is at stake in human being which is obscured, suppressed, disregarded, or distorted. How to penetrate the shell of his adjustments and to inquire whether adjustment is his ultimate vocation? We study human behavior; we must not disregard human bewilderment."[50]

We hear and say so many words, but they are like an engine that goes round in circles, with no forward motion! In Shakespeare's *Merchant of Venice*, this criticism was voiced by Bassanio, who skewered Gratiano as someone who "speaks an infinite deal of nothing, more than any man in all Venice. His reasons are as two grains of wheat hid in two bushels of chaff: you shall seek all day ere you find them, and when you have them, they are not worth the search."[51] Reason can rev and rev uselessly with arguments lacking real content. "Intelligence [...] is always tempted to deviate toward a game of concepts that it finds fascinating, but it fails to realize that in this way it has broken the bond that unites it to reality."[52]

So, proposing some concepts, even if they are correct and right, does not suffice; this will not conquer life and quench the thirst that characterizes it. Nor will a "religious discourse," a "mere accumulation of various disjointed ideas incapable of inspiring others,"[53] move and convince people today. In order to

50 A.J. Heschel, *Who is Man?* (Stanford, CA: Stanford University Press, 1965), 5.

51 William Shakespeare, *The Merchant of Venice*, Act I, Scene I.

52 François Varillon, *L'umiltà di Dio* [The humility of God] (Magnano (Bi): Qiqajon–Comunità di Bose, 1999), 30.

53 Francis, Apostolic Exhortation *Evangelii Gaudium*, 147.

escape from the mire of nihilism, it is not enough to have a religious vision or to speak of God, transcendence, or the divine. You can be culturally religious or even Christian, but beyond the words that are said and the values that are proclaimed, you can nonetheless experience the void of existence, even to the point of despairing. Abstract and moralistic preaching, be it religious or secular, will not save us from nothingness. As Evdokimov wrote, "Discourses no longer suffice. The clock of history marks the hour when it is no longer just a question of speaking about Christ, but, rather, of *becoming* Christ, a place of His presence and of His word."[54] Concepts, even when they are perfect, cannot produce even a shred of what can overcome nothingness. Gnosis in any form cannot compete against existential, concrete nihilism. It is not enough to change our concepts and broaden our intellectual knowledge.

Dostoevsky described in his unique way his intolerance of empty speaking devoid of real experience, "I've grown so sick [...] of this chattering to amuse oneself, of this incessant flow of commonplaces, always the same, that [...] I blush even when other people talk like that."[55] Von Balthasar articulated the reason for this intolerance that has become pervasive in our time and that we experience ourselves. "In a world that no longer has enough confidence in itself to affirm the beautiful, the proofs of the truth have lost their cogency. In

---

[54] Paul Nikolaevich Evdokìmov, *L'amore folle di Dio* [The mad love of God] (Cinisello Balsamo (Mi): San Paolo, 2015), 63.
[55] Fyodor Dostoevsky, *Crime and Punishment*, trans. Constance Garnett (Mineola, NY: Dover Publications, 2001), 119.

other words, syllogisms may still dutifully clatter away like rotary presses or computers which infallibly spew out an exact number of answers by the minute. But the logic of these answers [of these lines of reasoning, of these syllogisms] is itself a mechanism which no longer captivates anyone. The very conclusions are no longer conclusive."[56] We can say things that are even true, but if they do not happen in front of our eyes in the manner of a concrete beauty that attracts (as Saint Thomas said, "pulchritudo est splendor veritatis,"[57] beauty is the splendor of the truth), they no longer convince anyone, neither us nor others. In fact, as von Balthasar continued, "If the verum lacks that splendor which for Thomas is the distinctive mark of the beautiful, then the knowledge of truth remains both pragmatic and formalistic."[58]

b) Increased rule-following

Others think that the antidote to existential nihilism is *a system of ethics.* Thus there is a proliferation of appeals to duty, to "things to do" that can even result in obedience and obeisance promoting one's own survival and resulting in various advantages, but do not in

[56] Hans Urs von Balthasar, *The Glory of the Lord: A Theological Aesthetics,* vol. 1, *Seeing the Form,* trans. Erasmo Leiva-Merikakis (Edinburgh: T & T Clark, 1982), 19.

[57] "Pulchritudo consistit in duobus, scilicet in splendore, et in partium proportione. Veritas autem habet splendoris rationem et acqualitas tenet locum proportionis." Thomas Aquinas, *Commentum in Primum Librum Sententiarum,* distinctio III, quaestio II, expositio primae partis.

[58] Balthasar, *The Glory of the Lord: A Theological Aesthetics,* vol. 1, *Seeing the Form,* 138.

the least provide an answer to our unease and urgent need for meaning. "Lacking the meaning, there remains only the duty, a useless focus on duty that drags me further down toward the bottom,"[59] said our young friend, quoted earlier. This perception was expressed well by Tolstoy. "After such an awakening, Nekhludoff always made some rules for himself which he meant to follow forever after, wrote his diary, and began afresh a life which he hoped never to change again. 'Turning over a new leaf,' he called it to himself in English. But each time the temptations of the world entrapped him, and without noticing it he fell again, often lower than before."[60] A system of ethics, even when it can be shared, is not enough. Once again, von Balthasar reveals the underlying reason. "But if the *bonum* lacks that *voluptas* [the fascination that attracts us and enables an experience of fullness, of enjoyment] which for Augustine is the mark of its beauty, then the relationship to the good remains both utilitarian and hedonistic."[61]

We all know the fragility of any attempt to base the answer to the thirst for fulfillment and fullness on a moral effort, on our own measure of diligence. However, while we adults may have become used to the fact that our projects, life plans, and "things to do" fail to satisfy the need that comes from our innermost beings, for young people that perception of emptiness and hunger for meaning is searing, even when they

[59] See here, p. 13.
[60] Leo Tolstoy, *The Resurrection*, trans. Anthony Briggs (Empire Books: 2012), 67.
[61] Balthasar, *The Glory of the Lord: A Theological Aesthetics*, vol. 1, *Seeing the Form*, 152.

pretend not to notice, and they search for ways, often contradictory, to find fulfillment or at least to escape. In an article published a few months ago in *Corriere della Sera*, "Our Young People Die Fragile and Alone," Susanna Tamaro wrote, "Not a weekend passes without the sad news of groups of friends who lose their lives in a car crash after a night of partying in a club. New strategies are brought to bear to limit this tragic reality: more checks, breath analyzers at the exits of clubs, bus services that can bring young people home safe and sound. These measures are surely necessary and in part, do save lives, but they're not much different from fencing off the edge of a ravine with barbed wire. They will save some young people, but the ravine is still there [...]. What amazes me is that nobody stops to asks, after all these repeated events, what in the world is going on?"[62]

In front of this existential abyss, you cannot think that the answer is barbed wire. Rules, limits, and fences do not save life from the void. This cannot be the answer to the mystery of our being, and experience gives us continual confirmation of this. Nor do things change if with more refinement we turn to what the Greeks called "the golden mean," an ethics of the limit, to protect us from impulses, aspirations, and desires that are too great. As Galimberti wrote, "I would like this culture of the limit if it were drawn from our culture, which knows no limits to desire."[63]

---

[62] Susanna Tamaro, "Fragili e soli, così cadono i nostri ragazzi" [Our young people die fragile and alone], *Corriere della Sera*, October 18, 2019.

[63] Umberto Galimberti, "Il greco senso della misura" [The Greek sense of measure], *la Repubblica*, November 16, 2019, p. 182.

So is desire a defect to be corrected? In the face of its limitlessness, its excess, the fact that it never lets us be, it seems that from the ancient Greeks onwards, the one strategy employed has been to diminish it. But this more or less fierce struggle to confine it within acceptable limits is the most evident confirmation of its structural boundlessness, of its disturbing exorbitance. The failure of all attempts to bridle desire by imposing limits and rules shows just how irreducible it is; it demonstrates that deep down in our being, the Augustinian *cor inquietum* lives on.

c) Lowering the bar of desire

Attempts to reduce and mask desire are continual and capillary, as Luisa Muraro noted. "Objection and self-deception come with self-moderation: we settle for less. The self-deception begins when we begin to underestimate the enormity of our needs and start thinking we should make them commensurate to our strength, which is naturally limited." Consequently, we conform "to pretend desires like those in advertising, setting our sights on results of every kind; we no longer work for our true interest, no longer do what truly interests us, no longer seek what is to our [authentic] advantage; in practice, we end up working more to gain less."[64] We lower the bar of our desire, trying to fool our hearts. A young man wrote me, "It's hard for me to live up to my desire, and I often minimize it and settle for much less." Montale said, "One fills the void

[64] Luisa Muraro, *Il Dio delle donne [The God of women]* (Milan: Mondadori, 2003), 31–32.

with the useless,"[65] and elsewhere said, "Killing time necessarily means packing it with occupations to fill that void. Few people can look at that void without batting an eye, thus the social need to do something, even if this something barely anesthetizes the vague sense that the void will appear again in us."[66]

Is there anything more crucial today than discovering the original nature of our desire? As de Lubac observed, "The truly important thing to focus on is not the more or less burdensome tribute we all pay to human weakness, but the nature and extent of your desire."[67] The most insidious threat of our time is the failure to see and value the authentic stature of human desire; this failure can follow various roads and be promoted in various ways by those whose interests are served by controlling others' lives.

In his wisdom, C.S. Lewis had Screwtape articulate this concept: "The deepest likings and impulses of any man are the raw material, the starting-point, with which the enemy [God] has furnished him. To get him away from those is therefore always a point gained; even in things indifferent it is always desirable to substitute the standards of the World, or convention, or fashion, for a human's own real likings and dislikings."[68] This is the diabolical tactic: to distance us from

---

[65] Eugenio Montale, *Nel nostro tempo* [In our time] (Milan: Rizzoli, 1972), 18.

[66] Eugenio Montale, "Ammazzare il tempo" [Killing time], in *Auto da fè* (Milan: Il Saggiatore, 1966), 207.

[67] Henri de Lubac, "Ecclesia Mater," in *Meditazione sulla Chiesa* [Meditations on the church], vol. 8 of *Opera omnia* (Milan: Jaca Book, 1979), 188.

[68] C.S. Lewis, *The Screwtape Letters*, 78

our deepest impulses, from the desires that constitute us, distracting us. But distraction, used by every power to separate us from ourselves, shows its limits as soon as reality returns to shake us, as we have seen in this time of the coronavirus pandemic, bursting the bubble of our usual self-deception. With distraction, to use a line by the Italian rapper Marracash, which seems like an epitaph, "I fill the time, but not the emptiness."[69]

2. Our humanity

Unless something happens that can totally win over our being, reawakening interest in all of reality, every-thing becomes extraneous, as Joseph Roth wrote. "All of them were strangers one to another, imprisoned in a glass ball each one, unable to see or touch the oth-ers."[70] But neither mere discourses, be they secular or religious, nor appeals to duty, to "things to do," even in the name of religion, can redeem us deep down from the asthenia of desire and the numbing of interest we described earlier.

This is documented in the letter a young friend wrote me. "I discover in myself that the biggest temp-tation is to think I already know the answer to the question of 'what saves us from nothingness.' But in fact, I'm always on the edge of the void. Everything, even my girlfriend and my studies, even my degree,

[69] "TUTTO QUESTO NIENTE–Gli occhi" [ALL THIS NOTHING-NESS–The eyes], song by Marracash, 2019, © Universal Music.
[70] Joseph Roth, "The Blind Mirror," in *The Collected Stories of Joseph Roth*, trans. Michael Hoffman, 1st edition (New York: W. W. Norton & Company, 2002), 25.

can become boring, all alike and in some way distant [unable to satisfy desire]. Only afterwards do I become aware of this indifference [from which not even our relationships are exempt] and the more I look at it, the more it seems I'm coming into contradiction even with what I think I know. I realize that I'm surrounded by nothingness even in simply talking with fellow students: our conversations are marked by nothingness, and we pass from one topic to another without remembering what we were talking about before. But there is one thing I understand at moments like this: I'm not made for nothingness. What I need is not meaningless chatter, but something that grabs me and rips me away from the nothingness. However, it seems to me that just realizing this is not enough to face it."

Instead, I say, realizing that we are not made for nothingness is a crucial, indispensable element in the journey to identify what saves us from nothingness: the discovery of our human aspiration, of our humanity.

What is this humanity of ours that does not let us delude ourselves, that we cannot fool, that we cannot give just any arbitrarily chosen answer? Self-deception and distraction cover over the unease, but they do not save us from nothingness. Even though our humanity is in a bad way, wounded and muddled, it does not get confused, does not let the first person who passes by fool it, and this is the sign that it is less muddled than it may seem. Though at times, out of a lack of sincerity or attention or ultimate morality, we follow what is not true and allow ourselves to be dragged along by it, sooner or later the humanity in us makes us realize we have followed a great illusion, as expressed for example in François Furet's book, *The Passing of an Illusion: The Idea of Communism in the Twentieth Century.*

Our humanity is a critical and ultimately inescapable bulwark. We discover it in experience. "What I like about experience is that it is such an honest thing. You may take any number of wrong turnings; but keep your eyes open and you will not be allowed to go very far before the warning signs appear. You may have deceived yourself, but experience is not trying to deceive you. The universe rings true wherever you fairly test it."[71] However, in order for experience to be such, and here is the point, there must be a judgment, an evaluation, and therefore an underlying criterion as the basis for forming the judgment. What is the criterion? Our humanity. It is not simply something that makes us suffer, a burden we must carry in spite of ourselves, a bottomless pit that cannot be filled and that hinders our relationship with reality. No–it is our criterion for judgment.

I still remember how overjoyed I was when I consciously discovered in myself a capacity to judge that enables me to truly experience my relationship with everything. In fact, experience is what allows you judge what you undergo on the basis of the criterion of our humanity, which is a complex of original needs and evidences that structurally belongs to us and that is activated in a comparison with what we come across. I discovered that this complex of needs and evidences inside myself was the ultimate criterion for judging what happened.

[71] C.S. Lewis, *Surprised by Joy: The Shape of My Early Life* (London: Collins, 2012), 205.

Giussani's awareness of the cognitive importance of our humanity prompted him to say "only an attentive, tender, and impassioned awareness of my own self can make me open and lead me to acknowledge,"[72] that is, to perceive, what makes life worth living. We should ask ourselves whether the same passion, attention, and tenderness characterize our attitude toward ourselves. Sometimes this passion, attention, and tenderness almost seem like things from another galaxy. How moving to hear Giussani exclaim, "How human the human is, how human humanity is!"[73] How human my humanity is! Often we are afraid of our humanity rather than being passionate about it, and therefore we are confused, incapable of perceiving the truth, and in the end everything evaporates into abstraction. "He fell into a sort of deep abstraction, which could even be defined as torpor, and set off no longer paying attention to his surroundings, without even manifesting the desire to notice anyone."[74]

The more we suspend our humanity, the more we hesitate to recognize the value of what happens to us and become uncertain about the direction to take. This is the opposite of what the Spanish poet Jesús Montiel noted with emotion about his children during the coronavirus pandemic. "My children never fail to surprise me. During lockdown they never once complained, unlike us adults. They accept the situation because the true normality for children is their family. I observed

---

[72] Luigi Giussani, *At the Origin of the Christian Claim*, trans. Viviane Hewitt (Montreal: McGill-Queens's University Press, 1998), 6.

[73] Luigi Giussani, *Affezione e dimora* [Affection and dwelling place] (Milan: Bur, 2001), 42.

[74] Dostoevsky, *Crime and Punishment*, 19.

that a child who grows up in a loving home, which isn't necessarily perfect, doesn't wish for much more. […]. You are enough, they say. […] I believe that children are the proof that we're not made for projects, but for loving and being loved. Only in this way does the contingent situation make sense, and does the present not collapse."[75]

Children easily perceive what they need for living: the presence of their parents. We adults, paradoxically, balk and often slip into complaining. Obviously, there are adults who maintain and deepen the simple humanity of children. Etty Hillesum is a luminous example. In her *Diary* she wrote, "Oh God, I thank You for having created me as I am. I thank You for the sense of fulfilment I sometimes have; that fulfilment is after all nothing but being filled with You. I promise You to strive my whole life long for beauty and harmony and also humility and true love, whispers of which I hear inside me during my best moments."[76]

3. "The ability to feel with and for the whole person"

Do any of us have each day at least an instant of true tenderness for themselves, for our own humanity? So often we mistreat ourselves, get furious at our humanity, which, despite this, does not allow us to be seduced

---

[75] Jesús Montiel, *The Objective*, April 2, 2020.
[76] Etty Hillesum, *Etty: The Letters and Diaries of Etty Hillesum 1941-1943*, trans. Arnold Pomerans (Grand Rapids: William Eerdmans, 2002), 175.

by falsehood. We would prefer to escape from our humanity, but are unable to obliterate it. Nietzsche expressed this well in *The Gay Science*, in which his wanderer says, "This penchant and passion for what is true, real, non-apparent, certain—how it aggravates me!"[77]

For this reason I have always been struck by John Paul II's line, "Tenderness is the ability to feel with and for the whole person."[78] This "feel with" the whole person is essential for living and is the opposite of sentimentalism, but, as Giussani says, it is "rare to find people full of tenderness for themselves!"[79] We probably can count on one hand how many such people we know, and not even use all five fingers. Today, very often anger and violence against ourselves and others, and against reality, dominate.

Even so, we all want to experience this tenderness toward our own humanity, as Camus wrote in *Caligula*: "Everything seems so complicated. Yet, really, it's quite simple. If I'd had the moon, Drusilla, the world, happiness, if love were enough, all might have been different. You know, Caligula, that I could be tender. Tenderness! But where could I quench this thirst? What human heart, what god, would have for me the depth of a great lake? […] There's nothing in this world, or in the other, made to my stature. And yet I know, and you, too, know […] that all I need is for the impossible to be. The impossible! I've searched for it at the confines

[77] Friedrich Nietzsche, *The Gay Science*, trans. Walter Kaufman (New York: Vintage Books, 1974), 246.

[78] Karol Wojtyla, *Love and Responsibility*, trans. H.T. Willets (New York: Farrar, Straus & Giroux, 1981), 207.

[79] Luigi Giussani, *Un avvenimento di vita, cioè una storia* [An event of life, that is, a history] (Rome-Milan: Il Sabato, 1993), 457.

of the world, in the secret places of my heart [it is what everyone seeks]. […] I've stretched out my hands […]; see, I stretch out my hands, but it's always you I find, you only, […] like spit in my face. You in the splendid and sweet light of the stars […] you who are for me a wound I want to dig out with my fingernails."[80]

If we do not find "something" that enables us to have this tenderness toward our thirst, toward our humanity, we will end up seeing it as a wound, something to be freed of, exactly the opposite of love. But why would we want to be free of it? So as not to feel the drama, so as to dull it as much as possible, so as not to sense the inadequacy of everything we pin our hopes on, so as not to have to face the disproportion between what we desire and what we manage to obtain. As Camus said, "There's nothing in this world, or in the other, made to my stature" or as Guccini sang, referring to a love relationship, "You see dear, it's difficult to explain / it's difficult to understand if you haven't already understood // You're so much, but you're not enough, / […] you're everything, but that everything is still little."[81]

Thus the alternative is between tenderness ("the ability to feel with and for the whole person") and hatred of our own humanity ("a wound I want to be free of"). How often we worry because we are unable to suppress or compress our humanity. Notwithstanding all our efforts to silence it, when we least expect it, it explodes and makes itself felt.

[80] Albert Camus, *Caligula*, in *Caligula and Three Other Plays*, trans. Justin O'Brien (New York: Alfred Knopf, 1958), 73.
[81] "Vedi cara" [You see, dear], lyrics and music by Francesco Guccini, 1970, © EMI.

This experience is exemplified beautifully in *Miguel Mañara* by Milosz. Mañara abandons himself to dissolute living, but this fails to fill the abyss of his humanity and desire. "I have drawn Love into pleasure, into the mud, and into death; [...]. I eat the bitter herb of the rock of boredom; I have served Venus angrily, then maliciously, and disgustedly. [...]. Certainly in my young years, I too sought, just as you do, the miserable joy, the restless stranger who gives you her life without telling you her name. But the desire was soon born in me to pursue what you'll never know: a love immense, dark and sweet. [...]. Ah, how do I fill up this emptiness in life? What can I do? For the desire is always there, stronger and madder than ever. It's like a fire in the sea that blasts its flame into the deep universal black emptiness."[82] The desire remains, persists, stronger than ever, notwithstanding everything. This is the surprise, as we said. It does not die out. The more you live, and go through things, and try to satisfy it or deaden it, the more it grows.

As Augustine said, nothing is commensurate to the depth of the human heart, which vibrates in each of us. "If by abyss we understand a great depth, is not man's heart, do you not suppose, an abyss? For what is there more profound than that abyss? Men may speak, may be seen by the operations of their members, may be heard speaking in conversation: but whose thought is penetrated, whose heart is seen into? What he is inwardly engaged on, what he is inwardly capable of,

---

[82] O.V. Milosz, *Miguel Mañara,* trans. Crossroads Cultural Center, Comments by Luigi Giussani, 4, http://www.crossroadsculturalcenter.org/booklets/

what he is inwardly doing or what purposing, what he is inwardly wishing to happen, or not to happen, who shall comprehend? I think an abyss may not unreasonably be understood of man, of whom it is said elsewhere, 'Man shall come to a deep heart, and God shall be exalted.'"[83]

So then, we ask once again, What saves us from nothingness? What can fill this abyss of life, this irreducible desire, uncomfortable and sublime, "even greater than such a universe,"[84] sign of the human that is in us, that unmasks the incompleteness and insufficiency of our attempts?

[83] Saint Augustine, *Expositions on the Psalms*, 42:12, https://www.newadvent.org/fathers/1801042.htm
[84] Leopardi, *Pensieri* LXVIII, 113.

CHAPTER 3

"CARO CARDO SALUTIS"

"*Caro cardo salutis.*" (The flesh is the pivot of salvation.)[85] This line by Tertullian, a father of the church, may seem enigmatic but its meaning becomes clear as soon as we look at our experience. If and when we have been freed from nothingness, what was able to do it?

1. A presence in the flesh

A personal contribution to help us understand this theme comes from the following letter that a young woman sent me:[86] it focuses simply and clearly on the point that interests us, and I think others will easily identify with what she says, even if their own experiences took different forms.

"When I ask myself what saves me from nothingness, I can't help but thinking of my own story up to now. Two moments struck me particularly and come to mind when I think about this nothingness. One is the memory of the immense disproportion I felt as a child looking up at the stars. I was shocked to think

Tertullian, *De carnis resurrectione* [On the resurrection of the flesh], 8, 3: PL 2,806.
This refers to an invitation to send written responses to the question of what saves us from nothingness. See here, pp. 3-4.

that I was nothing compared to the immensity of the universe, so much so that some nights I couldn't sleep because my life seemed like a meaningless moment in the passage of time. The other moment happened as I was getting into the car with my mother to return home after shopping with her, something I usually really enjoyed, but this time I felt an infinite sadness, one that has always been part of my life. I told my mother, 'There are days when nothing in particular happened but I suddenly feel an enormous sadness and I don't know why.' We remained silent on the trip home, with the radio playing softly. An infinite sadness that ended in nothingness. When I transferred to a new school founded by some families in CL, I met the movement, and with it Christianity. A couple of years after the illness and death of my father, which happened when I was seventeen, I decided to receive my First Communion and to join the movement. In my first year at university I met a priest who saw that I was going through a painful period and gave me the letter you had written about sexual abuse, a situation that had nothing to do with what I was experiencing, but your words about the thirst for justice spoke to my thirst in general ("Wounded, We Return to Christ," *la Repubblica*, April 4, 2020). You said this thirst is 'boundless,' 'bottomless,' and 'is so infinite that it cannot be quenched.' 'If this is the situation, the most burning question, which nobody can avoid, is as simple as it is inexorable: "*Quid animo satis*?"' Why could you even ask this question? Why could you suppose that there was something that could fulfill and satisfy the soul? I read and reread the letter, sitting in my living room, and burst into tears, thinking, 'Is it really possible that this pain, this wound, can be healed and this desire for eternity can be fulfilled? Is there something in this world that can do these things? It was the first time in my life that I thought there might be something real, carnal, and concrete that could respond to my thirst. Suddenly it was as if all the pieces came together: the people I'd met at that school, the gaze my teachers had on the students, which was so different, and those moments at the summer camps when my heart swelled and I thought to myself, 'It's as if I've been waiting all my life to be told these things.' All this was a concrete 'You,' as big as my wound and my desire for eternity. 'Someone who makes the hereafter present in the here and now: Christ, the mystery made flesh.' These years have been the story of affection for this concrete flesh, a concrete 'You.' During these weeks of lockdown I've been realizing that Christ has won me over, making me see and experience that my sadness isn't condemned to nothingness."

But after encountering this carnal presence that saves us from nothingness, the game is not over because many events in life, or sometimes our own presumption or weakness, or difficulties that arise and disorient us, can cause us to lose our way and stray far from the presence that was encountered and to abandon it. In these cases as well, it will always and only be something in the flesh that seizes us again. A few months ago a university student wrote me, "A year ago, under the weight of certain things I kept inside me, I ran away from the companionship, even though I had recognized that it was essential for my life. I didn't know myself anymore. My outlook on life was dead and empty; my heart was so wearied that I just wanted to disappear. I believed there was nothing to be done for me, that there was no hope, and that I would never recover. But through the companionship of some friends who never left me alone, who took care of me and my heart, I tried to start again. I began again because those faces looked at me with a love and tenderness that I couldn't feel for myself."

How well our "detector" works in us! When a person is looked upon with such tenderness that embraces the whole "I," she realizes it immediately!

Her letter continues, "I've often asked myself why and how others can love me when I can't love myself. What heart do they have? What must they have seen? What must they have encountered to be able to love someone like me? I wanted to understand. So I began searching for the answer, and it was a full year, intense and strenuous, but very beautiful, a year that overturned and filled my life, not because I was so good or because the pain and fear inside me disappeared, but because I experienced through those concrete faces that 'unimagined, unimaginable correspondence to the heart.'[87] I want everyone to experience the beauty of such an encounter and friendship. It's so beautiful to live with the certainty of having found a great companionship for my heart, and I want to hold on tight and not let it go. I don't want to lose it and go back to my thoughts, because I realize now as never before that only in this place is everything about me, my weaknesses and fears, my pain and need, welcomed and

---

[87] Luigi Giussani, Stefano Alberto, and Javier Prades, *Generating Traces in the History of the World* (Montreal: McGill-Queen's University Press, 2010), 7.

loved. Only here can I look at myself and take myself seriously without leaving out anything, without taking anything for granted. I realize that only in this companionship do I find friends who love my heart. I'm amazed that I'm so certain, because normally I'm not this way."

When we encounter a gaze so full of true tenderness for us, we realize there is an alternative to our self-hatred and anger.

The letter continues, "So, what saves me from nothingness? What saved me from the nothingness of those days? This companionship." In other words, a real, carnal companionship in history. This is the flesh that saves life. *Caro cardo salutis*: the flesh, not our thoughts or imaginings or fantasies, not the virtual, but flesh, or as she concluded, "precise faces where I find this gaze of love and tenderness that direct me to another, a living 'You,' present here and now, faces that have brought me back to life."

"The flesh is the pivot of salvation." You recognize this flesh because it is different, as recounted in a moving autobiographical passage in Daniele Mencarelli's *The House of the Gazes*: "At the Liberty window there are two young parents. The mother is holding a child while the father plays with him, showing him the fountain in the inner garden and making his son laugh by making funny faces and sticking out his tongue. When I am no more than a yard from them the two parents turn and with them the child. My steps falter as does my breath. The little one is about three years old, and except for his eyes, he has no face. In the place of his nose and mouth there are holes of red flesh. I look down at the marble pavement and slip by without looking at them. [...] I dawdle and wait for those two young parents and their disfigured child to leave. The child's laughter arrives first. They're still there, but now they're not alone. In front of them is an old nun; she bends forward and gently touches her face to his appalling one. 'You're mamma and papa's beautiful boy, aren't you? She takes his little hand and kisses it; he bursts out laughing, maybe because it tickles. The nun is at least eighty years old and her chubby face is white as milk. 'Ah, you're not only beautiful, you're also a sweetie. Do you like this?' She passes his little hand over her mouth and chin, to please him. Then she stands upright and looks at the father and mother. 'Do you hear what a laugh he has? Inside this child there isn't silver, there's gold, living gold.' She kisses him, mindless of his face, of everything. I am stunned. I can't understand, can't process it. I've seen something so human and at the same time so foreign, like a rite from a faraway land. I can't find within me the tools for translating it into my language. [...] I've tried every approach possible. I've tried to liquidate what I saw as the delirium of an old woman clad in grey, then as the fanaticism of a nun deaf and blind to pain, who wanted at all costs to defend the supremacy of her God, even in front of that disfigurement, then as a stupendous actress who shortly after, maybe in the privacy of the bathroom, washed her mouth after having kissed that deformed face. But none of these readings can bridge the distance between what I saw and my logic."[88]

[88] Daniele Mencarelli, *La casa degli sguardi* [The house of the gazes] (Milan: Mondadori, 2020), 183–85.

The writer tried to explain the exceptional thing he had seen, that had invaded his vision ("something so human and at the same time so foreign"), that had attracted him and in a certain sense seized him; he tried to bring it down to the level of the known, the foreseeable, the comprehensible. How often we obstinately try to reduce the diversity that we see and bring it down to our measure! "Man is so loyal to systems and abstract deductions that he is ready to distort the truth intentionally, he is ready to deny the evidence of his sense only to justify his logic."[89]

What magnetized Mencarelli? The same thing that attracted the young women who wrote those letters: a human difference. In front of the completely disfigured face of that child, the nun did not draw back; rather, she felt a tenderness, a deep, dizzying, carnal fondness, a fondness in the most intense sense of the word, a vortex, an abyss of affection so deeply human that it appeared even more than human, "foreign," divine.

Only flesh, a carnal presence, can save us from nothingness, a presence that all our interpretations fail to negate, so much does it magnetize us, seize us, attract us all the way down to the core of our being, eliciting all our desire in the very moment when it makes us experience an unimaginable correspondence to it. Who would not want to be looked upon with the tenderness shown to the women who wrote those letters, or shown by that nun in looking at that child?

[89] Fyodor Dostoyevsky, *Notes from the Underground* (Mineola, NY: Dover Thrift Editions, 1992), 16. This is unabridged republication of the Constance Garnett translation of *Notes from the Underground,* as originally published in the collection *White Nights and Collected Stories* (New York: Macmillan Company, 1918).

Only an encounter with such an incarnate gaze can fill "the abyss of life" described by Milosz. Only flesh can vanquish nothingness. Not just any flesh, not just any carnal presence, but a presence that brings with itself something that corresponds to all our expectancy and therefore magnetizes our being. In fact, there is flesh that leaves a bitter taste and ends up in the boredom of a life of solitude, as happened to Miguel Mañara before his encounter with Girolama and the newness she brought into his life. As de Lubac wrote, "Nothing man creates or nothing that remains on the human level will be able to save him from solitude. Rather, solitude will continue to grow the more he discovers himself, because it is nothing other than the opposite of the communion to which he is called."[90]

2. The Jew Jesus of Nazareth

What can defeat the nihilism in us? Only being magnetized by a presence, by flesh that brings with itself, in itself, something that corresponds to all our expectancy, all our desire, all our need for meaning and affection, for fullness and for esteem. We will be saved from nothingness only by that flesh able to fill the "abyss of life," the "mad desire" for fulfillment in us, to use once again the words of Milosz.

If this experience does not happen, we do not leave behind our nihilism, even if we are culturally formed by religious discourses and make all kinds of efforts, because the "proofs of the truth" of which von

[90] De Lubac, "Ecclesia Mater," 35.

Balthasar spoke, and the many things for us to do, are incapable of seizing us and drawing in our whole "I." Sooner or later, usually sooner than later, they end up boring us.

This gaze full of tenderness for our humanity entered the world through the flesh of a man, the Jew Jesus of Nazareth, two thousand years ago. "In the incarnation, the eternal Logos has so bound himself to Jesus such that […] the Logos can no longer be thought apart from his connection to the man Jesus. […] Whoever comes into contact with the Logos touches Jesus of Nazareth. […] He is the Logos himself, who in the man Jesus is a historical subject. Certainly God touches man in many ways even outside of the sacraments. But he touches him always through the man Jesus, who is His self-mediation into history and our mediation into eternity."[91]

This event, the Incarnation, is a watershed in human history that can never be eliminated. For this reason Giussani said, "It is in flesh that we can recognize the presence of the Word made flesh; if the Word has become flesh, it is *in flesh* that we find Him."[92] Those who encounter it perceive they are in front of the most crucial event of their lives. We see it clearly when it happens. Let's go back then to one of the most significant episodes in the Gospels from this point of view, trying to identify with the situation of that woman who arrived in front of Jesus

---

[91] Joseph Ratzinger, *Christ, Faith and the Challenges of Culture*, Meeting with the Doctrinal Commissions of Asia, Hong Kong, March 3, 1993. https://www.vatican.va/roman_curia/congregations/cfaith/incontri/rc_con_cfaith_19930303_hong-kong-ratzinger_en.html
[92] Luigi Giussani, *L'attrattiva Gesù* [The attraction of Jesus] (Milan: Bur, 1999), 123. Cf. Dogmatic Constitution on the Divine Revelation *Dei Verbum*, 4.

painfully conscious of herself and her need, grieving for all her sins, unable to find peace or to see herself with any tenderness, maybe with an impulse to rip away her humanity and the desire that she had sought so maladroitly to satisfy. And yet precisely that humanity, that need to be loved and looked upon with truth, was what allowed her to discover the unforeseen; that is, the presence of Jesus.

"A Pharisee invited Him to dine with him, and He entered the Pharisee's house and reclined at table. Now there was a sinful woman in the city who learned that He was at table in the house of the Pharisee. Bringing an alabaster flask of ointment, she stood behind Him at his feet weeping and began to bathe His feet with her tears. Then she wiped them with her hair, kissed them, and anointed them with the ointment. When the Pharisee who had invited Him saw this he said to himself, 'If this man were a prophet, he would know who and what sort of woman this is who is touching him, that she is a sinner.' Jesus said to him in reply, 'Simon, I have something to say to you.' 'Tell me, teacher,' he said. 'Two people were in debt to a certain creditor; one owed five hundred days' wages and the other owed fifty. Since they were unable to repay the debt, he forgave it for both. Which of them will love him more?' Simon said in reply, 'The one, I suppose, whose larger debt was forgiven.' He said to him, 'You have judged rightly.' Then he turned to the woman and said to Simon, 'Do you see this woman? When I entered your house, you did not give me water for my feet, but she has bathed them with her tears and wiped them with her hair. You did not give me a kiss, but she has not ceased kissing my feet since the time I entered. You did not anoint my head with oil, but she anointed my feet with ointment. So I tell you, her many sins have been forgiven; hence, she has shown great love. But the one to whom little is forgiven, loves little.'"[93]

This is the "unprecedented realism" that Benedict XVI described when he wrote that "the real novelty of the New Testament lies not so much in new ideas as in the figure of Christ himself, who gives flesh and blood to those concepts."[94] I believe that each of us would want to be reached by such a gaze, no matter what we had done, no matter how we had led our lives.

What did that woman need in order to be seized by Christ's gaze? Only her humanity, bad off and wounded as it was, and as it is for all of us, really. When she encountered that man, her humanity even with all her mistakes was entirely magnetized, to the point that there was no stopping her, and that woman walked to that banquet past the hostility and disapproval of others to wash Jesus's feet with her tears. Giussani's way of helping us immerse ourselves in the Gospel story and the identification with those people is one of the most beautiful things he taught us. In fact, we often take these stories for granted, depriving them of their factual, historical, and vital importance. Instead, by returning time after time to the episodes of the Gospel, by immersing us in the events they describe, Giussani made us "see" how Jesus interacted with the wounded humanity, full of limits, of those He encountered. Nothing blocked Him then, and nothing blocks Him now. Without this humanity of ours, which so often irritates us because things are not the way we want, or because

93 Lk 7:36–47.
94 Benedict XVI, Encyclical Letter *Deus Caritas Est*, 12.

we dislike all the limitations we see in ourselves, Christ would not have a way to enter your and my life, would not have a point of connection. In fact, it is precisely our humanity that He turns to and seizes, all the way to our innermost depths. "Only God grasps the deep point of the conscience in which man, notwithstanding his own life and his own sins, is truly human and humanizes. Deep down, redemption is Christ, who draws upon that which is deepest in man, that which is of greater value than his sin,"[95] wrote François Varillon.

Christ's gaze reads inside us, in the depths of our desire for fullness. Pope Francis spoke of this recently, "We are born with a *seed of restlessness*. God wanted it this way. A restlessness to find fullness, restlessness to find God, often without even knowing that we have this restlessness. Our heart is restless and thirsty, thirsty for the encounter with God. It seeks Him, often taking the wrong road; it gets lost, then returns and seeks Him... And in turn, God thirsts for the encounter, so much so that He sent Jesus to encounter us, to come to us in this restlessness."[96]

Never has a human being felt so radically affirmed as have those who have been captured by the gaze introduced into history by this man, Jesus of Nazareth. Never has a woman been spoken to about her son with the same original tenderness, with the same totally positive affirmation of his destiny, beyond any conceivable success or failure. With this dizzyingly affirmative gaze Jesus said to the woman bathing His feet with her tears,

[95] François Varillon, *Traversate di un credente* [Crossings of a believer] (Milan: Jaca Book, 2008), 98.
[96] Francis, *Homily at Santa Marta*, April 26, 2020.

"Your sins are forgiven." The others at table said to themselves [in rebellion against a newness that challenged them], "Who is this who even forgives sins?" [they did not say it with wonder, but rejecting it, as if to say He was a blasphemer]. But He said to the woman [nobody changed His attitude toward her], "Your faith has saved you; go in peace."[97] This gaze will never be uprooted from the face of the earth, and therefore whatever we say about ourselves, whatever you say about yourself, is not the final word.

The sinful woman in the Gospel was not saved from nothingness by her own thoughts, intentions, or efforts. It was a presence who had such a passion and preference for her person, for her "I," that she was won over entirely. The entire course of her life was overturned and revolutionized by that encounter. She no longer cared about the way others looked at her because she was entirely defined by Jesus, by His gaze, by that presence in flesh and blood. In all her life, nobody had ever looked at her the way that man did. Otherwise she would not have entered that house, would not have bathed His feet with her tears or dried them with her hair. What experience must she have had, what certainty must she have felt, to challenge the Pharisees at that table and the whole city as she did! Without such certainty you end up at the mercy of your comments and those of others. Instead, our thoughts and those of others are overcome by that gaze, which no power in this world can eliminate. The thoughts have not been removed, but their capacity to block us has been inhibited.

[97] Lk 7:48–50.

We can say, with von Balthasar, that this is "a certainty based not on the human understanding's own power of conviction, but on the manifest evidence of divine truth. In other words, this certainty is founded not on having grasped, but on having been grasped." The Swiss theologian stressed that this "is a vital question for Christianity today." Faith will be credible for the world surrounding us only if Christianity "first regards itself as being worthy of belief. And it will only do this if faith, for Christians, does not first and last mean 'holding certain propositions to be true' which are incomprehensible to human reason and must be accepted only out of obedience to authority. In fact, while divine revelation is transcendent, through it, faith leads man to the understanding of what God is in truth and, in and alongside this understanding, faith also leads man to self-understanding."[98]

That woman's certainty and faith were based on "the manifested evidence of divine truth" in the incomparable gaze of Jesus, which made her feel totally affirmed and seized, and on the experience of a correspondence to her constitutive needs, one she never before experienced. So powerful and resplendent is this evidence of the truth, that "such a revelation of glory needs no justification but itself."[99] The same awareness of how crucial this evidence is for the credibility of the faith today characterized the educational engagement of Fr. Giussani from the very beginning. "I was deeply convinced that, unless faith could be found and located in present expe-

---

[98] Balthasar, *The Glory of the Lord: A Theological Aesthetics*, vol. 1, *Seeing the Form*, 134–40.
[99] Ibid., 410. Cf. DS 3008.

rience, and confirmed by it, and useful for responding to its needs, it would not be able to endure in a world where everything, *everything*, said and says the opposite."[100]

3. An event

In Jesus of Nazareth, God became one of us. "The Word became flesh, and made His dwelling among us."[101] In order to understand what we are talking about, we necessarily have to return to the beginning and look attentively at what happened. In fact, our "know-it-already" attitude often alters our comprehension. "Let's put ourselves in those times. Nobody knew about Jesus Christ. His name had not become a commonplace. What they saw was a man," who walked the streets, whom you could meet, with whom you could talk. Jesus was a contemporary presence in the life of Peter, Zacchaeus, and Mary Magdalene. "In listening to that man, there was a new presentiment of life; you didn't even articulate it to yourself, you just sensed it." And then, "there was an evening when for Peter, for Zacchaeus, for Mary Magdalene, in that day, something had happened that was and continued to be their whole life": they came upon that man and were seized, magnetized by Him. That was the crucial event for them. In fact, in that man "the eternal, substance, being, meaning, that which makes them worthwhile, finally the

---

[100] Luigi Giussani, *The Risk of Education: Discovering Our Ultimate Destiny*, trans. Mariangela Sullivan (Montreal McGill-Queen's University Press, 2019), xxxii.
[101] Jn 1:14.

object for whom reason is made, for whom consciousness is made, for whom the 'I' is made, makes itself present. Substance, permanence, totality is a man!"[102]

And for us two thousand years later? It is the same, identical. Speaking to university students, Giussani said, "What led us here today may have been a fleeting, subtle presentiment of promise for life, without any earth-shattering self-awareness or insight. But there was a day in your life when an encounter happened that encompassed all the meaning, value, desirableness, all the justness, beauty, and pleasantness. Because God- made-man is this. And God-made-man reaches you with hands, eyes, a mouth, with the physical reality of a humanity."[103] What reality? That of the company of believers in Him, His mysterious body. The man who said, "I am the way, the truth and the life"[104] rose from the dead and is contemporary with history. "I am with you always, until the end of the age."[105] Where do we see Him? Where do we hear Him? His presence here and now coincides with a visible, tangible, concrete phenomenon comprised of people who have been reached by His initiative and who have acknowledged Him: it is the reality of the church. "Christ's relevance for people of all times is shown forth in his body, which is the Church."[106]

"Even when Jesus was at the height of his earthly activity, the event that He was assumed an identifiable

[102] Luigi Giussani, *Qui e ora (1984-1985)* [Here and now] (Milan: Bur, 2009), 425–27.
[103] Ibid., 426.
[104] Jn 14:6.
[105] Mt 28:20.
[106] John Paul II, Encyclical Letter *Veritatis Splendor*, 25.

form that was not merely his external, physical appearance, but also that of those who believed in him; so much so that they were sent by him to convey his words–his message–to reproduce his prodigious acts, to bring the salvation that *his* person was."[107]

Christ is a contemporary presence, and recognition of this happens through the identical experience of two thousand years ago, as documented in the two letters quoted and the passage by Mencarelli; namely, the impact with the presence of a different humanity that evokes a new presentiment of life. It strikes us because it corresponds like nothing else to our structural thirst for meaning and fullness. Then and now, it is the experience of an encounter that "encompasses all meaning, value, desirableness, justness, beauty, and pleasantness," as Giussani put it. This is the way we are bowled over by His presence now. "To encounter means to come across something different that attracts us because it corresponds to our heart. So it is subjected to the comparison and the judgment of reason, and causes freedom to come forth in affection."[108]

Giussani characterized the presence of this human difference as "exceptional," not in the sense of superior individual performance, strangeness, or eccentricity, but in the correspondence of which we spoke before. You can define something as exceptional when it corresponds adequately to the original expectancy of the heart, even if you may not have a clear awareness of it. Why should something that "corresponds" be consid-

---

[107] Luigi Giussani, *Why The Church?* trans. Vivianne Hewitt (Montreal: McGill-Queen's University Press, 2001), 21.
[108] Giussani, Alberto, and Prades, *Generating Traces*, 18.

ered "exceptional"? Because the correspondence to our original needs, which should be normal, usually does not happen. Today we can understand it better than ever: we have everything, we have access to everything in every sense of the word much more than before, incomparably more, in terms of relationships, things, and experiences, but none of this can seize us deep down and make us experience the correspondence for which our heart thirsts. Therefore, when this correspondence happens in a certain encounter, it is something exceptional. The presence, the face through which we experience the correspondence, differs from others precisely in this, and we say, "it's exceptional!"

Only the contemporaneousness of Christ can save us from nothingness. Only His presence here and now can be the adequate response to nihilism, to the void of meaning, a presence not in spiritualistic terms, abstractly "ideal," but carnal and historical. Christ is not an idea or a thought, but a real event that bursts into my life. I encounter "something that has something within"[109] and that magnetizes my being. "Jesus Christ, that man of two thousand years ago, is immanent, becomes present, under the veil, under the aspect of a different humanity."[110]

Another letter offers us a vivid documentation of this. "I never thought that on the cusp of fifty someone

[109] Luigi Giussani, *The Journey to Truth Is an Experience*, trans. John Zucchi and Patrick Stevenson (Montreal: McGill-Queen's University Press, 2006), 96.
[110] Luigi Giussani, "Something That Comes First," Notes from the Assembly of CL Responsibles, January 1993, *Traces*, "Page One," November 11, 2018, https://english.clonline.org/traces/page-one/something-that-comes-first

could be born again. I lived for forty-seven years convinced that Jesus Christ was not indispensable for me.
All these years I pursued objectives that did not stand
up to the test of time: the university, my profession, my
family. Each time I achieved one of my goals I didn't
feel satisfied and I always went in search of new objectives. While most people thought I had a beautiful life, I
sensed that I was nourishing myself with something that
didn't sate me. All this generated a deep crisis: I felt useless and my relationships with friends, colleagues and
loved ones began to be difficult. I wanted to be alone.
One day, through my children's school, I met a person
whose eyes were radiant. He, too, was going through a
time that was not easy because of problems at work, but
he appeared serene and self-confident to me, in other
words, glad. I didn't know what enabled him to be this
way, nor did I know he was in CL. We became good
friends and this made me want his company. We went
on vacation together with our respective families and I
became more curious about him. I began to spend time
with his friends, who then became my friends. I started
participating in the gestures of the movement. I began
to pray again, to go to Mass and confession. At times I
asked myself why I was doing this, and my answer was
that it made me feel better. To this day I'm surprised by
this friendship, rooted in love for Jesus Christ. Before,
I only had friends with whom I shared work, passion
for the same sport, or mutual advantage. These three
years have changed and improved me. Those who have
known me a long time, old friends, family members,
and colleagues, have noticed something different about
me. Maybe it's not the same light that's in my friend's
eyes, but I believe that sporadically a glimmer shows in

mine, too. I want to be more in contact with this group of friends, to be reminded that "Christ is everything," as Fr. Giussani said, to be helped to recognize "He who is among us" and to "live this consciousness," being reminded of it "until it becomes a habit."[111]

This is the method by which faith is and will always be communicated: an unforeseeable encounter that kindles desire and moves the person to verify the promise that it brings by participating in the life of the Christian community. "The early church, after the end of the apostolic time, developed a relatively reduced missionary activity; she had no strategy for announcing the faith to the pagans [...] and yet even so this time became a period of great missionary success. The conversion of the ancient world to Christianity was not the result of a planned action but of the proof of the faith in the world as it was made visible in the life of Christians and in the community of the church. Humanly speaking, the real invitation from experience to experience, and nothing more, was the missionary power of the early church. The community of life of the church invited others to participate in this life, which revealed the truth from which this life came [...]. Only the interweaving of a truth consequent in itself and a guarantee of the life of this truth can make that evidence of faith desired by the human heart shine forth; only through this door does the Holy Spirit enter into the world."[112]

[111] Luigi Giussani, *The Work of the Movement: The Fraternity of Communion and Liberation* (Milan: Cooperativo Nuovo Mondo, 2006), 220.
[112] Joseph Ratzinger, *Guardare Cristo: Esercizi di Fede, Speranza e Carità* [Looking at Christ: Meditations on faith, hope and love] (Milan: Jaca Book, 1989), 31.

Nihilism/carnality: these terms define our situation today, and not only today but always, because the nihilism
we are describing is not a temporary phenomenon, but
rather a permanent possibility for the human soul, albeit
captured in different words at different times. Nihilism,
the nothingness that pervades us and to which we are
always tempted to yield, cannot be countered with mere
discourses, rules, or distractions, because they cannot
magnetize us and truly win over our humanity. This is
why Pope Francis stresses the danger of reducing Christianity to Gnosticism or Pelagianism.[113] The only thing
that responds to nihilism and the void of meaning,
both yesterday and today, is flesh, a gaze incarnate in
an eighty-year-old nun or in a friend. "Only Christ
takes my humanity so completely to heart."[114] Either I
experience today a presence that takes all my humanity completely to heart, or basically there is no escape,
because none of the discourses, systems of ethics, or
distractions available to us can generate the fullness
that I await from the depths of my being.

Without the experience of my "I" being seized there
is no Christianity; there is no Christianity as event,
that is, according to its original nature, and thus there
is no chance of change in how we conceive of and treat
people and things, no *metanoia* and no true affection.
"To be recognized, God entered man's life as a man in
a human form, so that man's thought, imagination, and
affectivity were, in a way, 'blocked,' magnetized by Him.
The Christian event has the form of an encounter, a

[113] Francis, *Evangelii Gaudium*, 94.
[114] Giussani, Alberto, and Prades, *Generating Traces*, ix.

human encounter in ordinary day-to-day reality."[115] Nothing is more intelligible for people and easier to understand than an event that takes place as an encounter. Thus one understands why Pope Francis often proposes this line from *Deus Caritas Est*: "I never tire of repeating those words of Benedict XVI which take us to the very heart of the Gospel: 'Being a Christian is not the result of an ethical choice or a lofty idea, but the encounter with an event, a Person, which gives life a new horizon and a decisive direction.'"[116] This is the method of God, the method God chose to save me, you, each of us, from nothingness, from the impossibility of fulfillment, from the suspicion that everything ends up in nothingness, from melancholic disappointment in oneself, from the easy descent into resignation and despair. "Everything in our life, today as in the time of Jesus, begins with an encounter."[117]

God became flesh and dwells among us. This is Christianity. It is not primarily a doctrine or a morality, but One present, here and now. The rest, the doctrine and morality, comes later. "He who made all things [that is, God–the origin, destiny, and meaning of life] identified with the precariousness of flesh, [still] identifies with the precariousness of flesh, makes Himself heard and tangible in the precariousness of flesh,"[118] that of people like you and me, flesh that is fragile and full of limits but has been seized

[115] Ibid., 17.
[116] Francis, *Evangelii Gaudium*, 7.
[117] Francis, *Address to the Communion and Liberation Movement*, Saint Peter's Square, March 7, 2015.
[118] Luigi Giussani, *La verità nasce dalla carne* [Truth is born of the flesh] (Milan: Bur, 2019), 115.

and made different. If Christianity has fascinated us, if we share a bond with a certain reality, it is because we have seen people engaged in a different way with everyday things, with a gladness and a peace, even in pain and difficulties. It is a way of engagement that we desired for ourselves–with a gratuitousness and positivity of gaze even in front of the most difficult and contradictory circumstances–so that we found that we envied them. They were people seized and changed by the Christian event, which for them had the form of an encounter; they were witnesses to a newness of life that shakes up the environment around them. The origin of this effect is well described in the Ambrosian liturgy: "I will make my presence evident in the gladness of their heart."[119]

Therefore, Giussani observed, if God became flesh in Jesus, "you must be in the flesh to understand Jesus. Experience is what enables us to understand Jesus. If God, the mystery, became flesh, born of the womb of a woman, you cannot understand anything of this mystery unless you start out from material experiences. If in order to be understood God became flesh, you must start from the flesh." He continued, "If you leave out the flesh, you destroy the paradox: this faith interests no one,"[120] and becomes mere discourse, becomes abstract, becomes ethics, becomes a

---

[119] "Populus Sion, ecce Dominus veniet ad salvandas gentes: et auditam faciet Dominus gloriam laudis suae in laetitia cordis vestri," Confractory of the IV Sunday of Advent, in *Messale ambrosiano: Dall'Avvento al Sabato Santo* [Ambrosian missal: From Advent to Holy Saturday], Milan, 1942, p. 78.
[120] Luigi Giussani, *Si può (veramente?!) vivere così? [Is It (Truly) Possible to Live This Way?]* (Milan: Bur, 2011), 481, 207.

user's manual, and no longer magnetizes us. Only a human experience allows you to discover the presence of Christ, to understand what a relationship with Him is.

4. To perceive the truth, all that is needed is sincere attention

It is easy to perceive the contemporary presence of Christ. The presences that magnetize us and make us experience the correspondence of which we have spoken are rare, and therefore, perceiving them is easy. For Peter, Zacchaeus, the Samaritan woman at the well, and Mary Magdalene it was easy. It is easy, but it is not necessarily taken for granted. This was seen with Jesus, too. Just think of how scandalized and disgusted people were when He went to Zacchaeus's home.

What was in Peter, Zacchaeus, the Samaritan woman at the well, Mary Magdalene and the others who encountered Him, that enabled them to perceive His newness, His difference, His uniqueness? Sincere attention, a gaze wide open. In fact, "finding the ultimate truth is like discovering something beautiful along one's path. One sees and recognizes it, if one is attentive. The issue, then, is this attention."[121] It is within the grasp of everyone, and this is liberating because it frees the field of a common objection that disguises disengagement with the reality of life and goes something like: "I'm not able. I'm not intelligent. I don't have the means for understanding." To perceive the truth, all you need is attention.

[121] Giussani, *The Religious Sense*, 34.

Certainly, it is never easy to pay attention, as Simone Weil wrote, "Something in our soul has a far more violent repugnance for true attention than the flesh has for bodily fatigue. [...] Attention consists of suspending our thought, leaving it detached, empty, and ready to be penetrated by the object."[122] But in order to let your thought be penetrated by the object, in order not to be closed in on your own measure, in order to "to be wide open toward the totality of factors at play,"[123] you must have a glimmer of affection for yourself, some sliver of interest in the destiny of your own existence. This glimmer, even if it is down in the depths of the soul, enables us to accept that we are loved, to pay attention to and react to a presence that affirms our being.

Peter, Zacchaeus, the Samaritan woman at the well, and Mary Magdalene did not reduce their humanity. Their gaze expressed the thirst and restless, suffering expectancy evoked by the presence of that man. He embraced and corresponded to this expectancy, and in doing so, caused it to reverberate all the more. Certainly, the exceptional presence of Jesus inspired that wide-open gaze, but they had to follow up on that inspiration; nothing happened magically or mechanically (for it if did, it would have been extraneous to their humanity).

---

[122] Simone Weil, *Waiting on God* (New York: Routledge, 2010), 56.
[123] Giussani, *The Religious Sense*, 126. The entire passage in which this line is contained reads: "To summarize, educating one's freedom to attentiveness, that is, to be wide open toward the totality of factors at play, and educating it to acceptance, that is, to the conscious embrace of what it finds before it is the fundamental issue of the human journey." In this way, Fr. Giussani addresses the essential problem of *educating* one's freedom to attentiveness.

Thus a living humanity and attention and reason affectively engaged are necessary for perceiving presences that bring a newness of life. There cannot be attention and a wide-open reason without affective vibration and interest. An attentive gaze is always a gaze full of interest. "If a certain thing does not interest me, then I do not look at it; if I do not look at it, then I cannot know it. In order to know it, I need to give my attention to it. In its Latin root, attention means 'to be tensed toward ...' If it interests me, strikes me, I will be 'tensed toward' it when faced with it."[124]

5. A recognition called faith

Therefore, this attention is the beginning of a recognition of the nature of what we have in front of us. In fact, in perceiving a presence of a different humanity when and where it happens, it is difficult to suppress a question about the nature of what you see. In front of the presence of Jesus, the people who heard Him speak or saw Him act were moved to ask "Who is this man?" This strange question was evoked by His irreducible difference. "They know where he comes from, they know his mother and his relatives, everyone knows about him, but the power shown by the man is so disproportionate, his personality is so great and so different that even the question has a different meaning: Who is this man?"[125]

---

[124] Ibid., 29.
[125] "Cristo la compagnia di Dio all'uomo" [Christ, God's companionship with man], Easter Poster, 1982, Communion and Liberation.

Today we wonder the same thing about people we have happened upon, gotten to know, and become friends with: "Who are you? Why are you this way?" These questions arise because their presence has something exceptional about it that becomes evident in our experience. This is how Christianity is communicated, then and now. The letter from the fifty-year-old expresses this well. In fact, asking these questions is symptomatic of the exorbitant problems posed by those who had dealings with Jesus. As Pope Francis observed, "Testimony evokes wonderment, and wonderment evokes questions in those who see it. People are moved to ask, 'Why in the world is this person this way? Where does this gift of hope come from? Where does this ability to treat others with charity come from?'"[126]

Does everyone look at you with the same tenderness? Does everyone look at you with the same gratuitousness? Does everyone look at you with the same passion for your destiny? Is everything equal? For this reason, when you find yourself in front of incomparable differentness, like the writer Mencarelli in front of that old nun, you cannot help asking, "Who *is* this person?" This amazed reaction that evokes an insuppressible question is the beginning of that journey of knowledge and recognition that is called faith.

Let's look at how it unfolded in the first people who encountered Jesus. Let's try to immerse ourselves in one of the many scenes of the Gospel, to look at the dynamic of knowledge that emerges from the story. Jesus

---

[126] Francis, *Senza di Lui non possiamo far nulla* [Without him we can do nothing] (Vatican City: LEV), 37.

and His disciples are walking to the region of Cesarea, and along the road He stops and asks them, "Who do people say that I am?" A bit surprised by His question, they try to answer. "Some say John the Baptist, others Elijah, and others Jeremiah or one of the prophets." Then Jesus asks them directly and personally, "Who do you say that I am?" The first to answer is Peter, with his usual impulsivity. "You are the Christ, the Son of the Living God."[127] How could he have said those words? Peter did not say something he arrived at through his own powers of reasoning: he repeated what he had heard Jesus say about Himself. They are not his words, reached on his own. Why does he repeat them? What made it fully reasonable to repeat them, even if he did not fully understand them? It was the certainty that Peter had reached about that man, the experience in a relationship with Him that made it evident that "if I can't trust this man, I can't even trust myself!"

6. Freedom and trust

Why was Peter able to trust Jesus? Why did he *have to* trust Jesus? ("If we don't believe in this man, we can't trust our own eyes either.") First of all, it is important to point out that the more we are attentive to a person's life, the more we are able to be certain about him or her. Who was able to understand that Jesus was to be trusted? The people who followed Him and spent time with Him, not those of the crowd who went to Him for healing but did not commit themselves to total in-

[127] Cf. Mt 16:13–19.

volvement with Him. You can gather the signs needed to reach certainty about a person only by spending time and sharing your life with that person. Then you can reasonably say "I can trust this person."

But the understanding and interpretation of signs demands freedom. Signs do not impose a conclusion even if they lead to it. "Freedom is exercised in that playing field called sign. [...]The sign is an event to *interpret*."[128] Different people interpreted Jesus in different ways, and in front of signs, freedom becomes evident.[129]

For many, freedom is a problem, because they perceive it as something that burdens life or weakens the truth of any conclusion they reach.

I was trying to explain to a young friend that freedom is not only something we cannot avoid, but that it is a good for us, and I gave him this example. I said, "Imagine that after spending some years with your girlfriend and noting many signs of the good you bring to each other, you decide to ask her to marry you. Would you be a little afraid to ask her?" He said, "I believe so." "But if everything was clear to you, why would you be worried?" I asked. He answered right away, "Because she might say no." "So you would be worried because you don't know whether all those signs would be sufficient for her to say yes? You would be vulnerable to her interpretation of the signs, or in other words, to her freedom. Is that right?" "Yes," he confirmed. At this point I asked him, "Would you prefer that it all

---

[128] Giussani, *The Religious Sense*, 123.
[129] Sulla libertà nell'atto di fede [On Freedom in the Act of Faith], cf. DS 3035.

be mechanical and automatic, so you wouldn't have to run the risk of her freedom and fear her saying no, or would you like her to say yes freely?" He said, "I'd prefer her to tell me freely, without a doubt." So I added, "Do you think God derives less pleasure than you from a freely given yes? God prefers a freely given yes too." Recently Pope Francis spoke about this as well. "How does Jesus act? [...] He respects, respects our own situation, and He doesn't rush ahead. [...] The Lord does not pick up the pace; He always goes at our pace, [...] and waits for us to take the first step."[130] This does not mean that He does not give us signs, all the signs we need, but we are free in front of them. God created us free and in some way submitted Himself to the decision of our freedom because there is no comparison between a freely said yes and mere acquiescence without the conscious exercise of freedom. I concluded, "If she said yes but it wasn't the fruit of her freedom, there would be no explosion of joy in you."

How crucial it is to realize that our freedom is not a complication, but a gift!

Thus, freedom is involved in the interpretation of signs that allows me to be fully reasonable in reaching the certainty that I can trust someone else. This confidence allowed Peter to make his own the words he had heard Jesus say. Faith is not a leap into the void: it is not an unreasonable act. "Faith means to recognize that what a historical presence says of itself is true. [...] A Man said something about Himself that others accepted as true, and that I, too, accept because of the exceptional way in which that fact still reaches me. Jesus

---

[130] Francis, *Homily at Santa Marta*, April 26, 2020.

is a man who said, 'I am the way, the truth and the life.' […] Paying attention to what that Man did and said to the point of saying, 'I believe in this Man,' adhering to His Presence, and affirming what He said as the truth: this is faith. Faith is an act of reason moved by the exceptional nature of a Presence that brings man to say, 'This man who is speaking is truthful. He is not lying, I accept what He says.'"[131] As the Catechism says, *"'To believe' has thus a twofold reference: to the person, and to the truth: to the truth, by trust in the person who bears witness to it."*[132]

Faith is the recognition of something that goes beyond reason's ability to grasp: the presence of the divine in the human. Reason alone could not define it, and yet it is a fully reasonable recognition that explains what I have in front of my eyes, the experience I have. As von Balthasar observed, there is an "interconnectedness of faith and the experience of fulfillment."[133]

"Faith is having the sincerity to recognize, the simplicity to accept, and the affection to cling to such a Presence. Sincerity and simplicity are analogous words. To be simple means to look something in the face, without bringing in extraneous factors borrowed from outside. […] We must look at the event for what it says, for what it communicates to reason, what it communicates to the heart, without bringing in external factors to evaluate it, for they have nothing to do with it."[134] You can say that simplicity means submitting

---

[131] Giussani, Alberto, and Prades, *Generating Traces*, 16.
[132] *Catechism of the Catholic Church*, n. 177.
[133] Balthasar, *The Glory of the Lord: A Theological Aesthetics*, vol. 1, *Seeing the Form*, 133.
[134] Giussani, Alberto, and Prades, *Generating Traces*, 21.

reason to experience, without introducing anything extraneous. The way Giussani spoke of this in front of the pope in Saint Peter's Square in 1998 will remain alive in our memory: "It was a simplicity of heart that made me feel and recognize Christ as exceptional, with that certain promptness that marks the unassailable and indestructible evidence of factors and moments of reality, which, on entering the horizon of our person, pierce us to the heart."[135]

[135] Ibid., x.

CHAPTER 4

A ROAD THAT LASTS ALL YOUR LIFE LONG

Once we have had the encounter and experienced being magnetized and seized by the presence of a different humanity in which we have recognized, according to our own time and following our own stories, the presence of Christ here and now, once we have begun to see the fruit of this encounter in our lives, we may think we have arrived and thus need journey no further. However, we have to admit that this is not so.

The encounter happens over and over and is renewed continually. It is the continual opening of a road that never stops being traveled. "This 'given' that has somehow crashed into our life becomes the point of departure for a *journey* [...]. That which has been given becomes the point of departure for a search, for a work that is absolutely the opposite of a dynamic of possession; rather, it is the labor of a desire that will never cease learning."[136]

1. The need for a journey

As soon as we stop journeying, believing we possess what has been given to us, heaviness and aridity in-

---

[136] Michel De Certeau, *Mai senza l'altro* [Never without the other] (Magnano (Bi): Qiqajon–Comunità di Bose, 1993), 26–27.

vade our days. Instead of flowers in our hands, we find dry grass. Once again, we see nothingness infiltrating into the fabric of our time, and feel surprised and disappointed. Why this aridity? More than ever, in those moments, these words of Etty Hillesum are ours: "My heart was once again frozen and would not melt; every outlet was blocked and my brain squeezed by a large vice."[137]

What happens to us? We experience what Ratzinger said about Saint Augustine. "When Augustine was converted in the garden at Cassiciacum he understood conversion according to the system of the revered master Plotin and the Neo-Platonic philosophers. He thought that his past sinful life would now be definitively cast off; from now on the convert would be someone wholly new and different, and his further journey would be a steady climb to the ever purer heights of closeness to God. It was something like that which Gregory of Nyssa described in his *Ascent of Moses*: 'Just as bodies, after having received the first push downwards, fall effortlessly into the depths with ever greater speed, so, on the contrary, the soul which has loosed itself from earthly passion rises up in a rapid upward movement... constantly overcoming itself in a steady upward flight.'"[138] We, too, maybe without realizing it, often conceive of what happened to us (the encounter, "conversion") according to frameworks developed elsewhere, far from our own circumstances. Ratzinger

[137] Etty Hillesum, "September 4, 1941," in *Etty: The Letters and Diaries of Etty Hillesum*, 92.
[138] Joseph Ratzinger, *Presentation by His Eminence Card. Joseph Ratzinger on the Occasion of the First Centenary of the Death of Card. John Henry Newman*, Rome, April 28, 1990.

continues: "Augustine's actual experience was a different one. He had to learn that being a Christian is always a difficult journey with all its heights and depths. The image of *ascensus* is exchanged for that of *iter*, whose tiring weight is lightened and borne up by moments of light which we may receive now and then. Conversion is the *iter*, the roadway of a whole lifetime. And faith is always *development*, and precisely in this manner it is the maturation of the soul to truth, to God, who is more intimate to us than we are to ourselves."[139]

Ratzinger formulated these observations on the occasion of the centenary of the death of John Henry Newman, now recognized as a saint, to underline the English cardinal's different and truer conception of conversion. "In the idea of 'development' Newman had written his own experience of a never finished conversion and interpreted for us, not only the way of Christian doctrine, but that of the Christian life. The characteristic of the great Doctor of the Church, it seems to me, is that he teaches not only through his thought and speech but also by his life, because within him, thought and life are interpenetrated and defined. If this is so, then Newman belongs to the great teachers of the Church, because he both touches our hearts and enlightens our thinking."[140]

We need to treasure and put into practice the precious contribution contained in these passages of Ratzinger. "Conversion is the *iter*, the roadway of a whole lifetime." "Faith is always '*development*.'" These words are also echoed in the persuasive prose of Péguy.

[139] Ibid.
[140] Ibid.

"Nothing is gained forever. This is the human condition itself. And the most profound condition of the Christian. The idea of an eternal gain, the idea of a gain that is definitive and will no longer be contested, is all that is most contrary to Christian thought. The idea of a dominion that is eternal and definitive and that will no longer be disputed is all that is most contrary to the destiny of human beings, in the system of Christian thought."[141]

Baptism as well, even though it introduces something irreducibly and definitively new in us, marking a watershed between the "before" and the "after," is only a beginning, the beginning of the battle that Christ wages to win over our existence, in the role of a *vir pugnator*, to "invade" it and in this way fulfill it. "With this objective fact [of baptism], that calls man to understand and accept to be part of the Event of Christ – in the church, baptism is always "seen as connected with faith: [...] the apostles and their collaborators offer Baptism to anyone who believed in Jesus";[142]]–"a new man is born, a new people."[143]

But "this beginning, set in time, could eventually be buried under a thick blanket of earth or in a tomb of forgetfulness and ignorance," as happens to many people. By encountering "a living Christian companionship"[144] we become aware of the extent of baptism and discover its fruit in our lives. Through our belonging

---

141 Charles Péguy, *Notes on Bergson and Descartes: Philosophy, Christianity, and Modernity in Contestation*, trans. Bruce K. Ward (Eugene OR: Cascade Books, 2019), 209.
142 *Catechism of the Catholic Church*, n. 1226.
143 Giussani, Alberto, and Prades, *Generating Traces*, 46.
144 Ibid.

to the life of this companionship, the grace of baptism develops in us.

Once again, a journey is involved. In fact, even those who have been chosen and touched through the gesture of baptism can "drown in the muddy ocean of the world, yielding to forgetfulness, not living the memory that is the awareness of Christ's presence, a real Event in the life of man."[145]

So there is no interruption in the journey. But the evidence that conversion is a lifelong journey and that faith is always development can make us yield, almost without realizing it, to the temptation to change our method; that is, in front of the needs of life, its personal and social challenges, we may be induced to substitute something else for the encounter. In other words, there is the temptation to take the event and faith for granted and set our sights elsewhere: we may want to seek the fulfillment of our life somewhere else and not in the event that attracted us. This is why Giussani wrote that "event" is "the word that the modern mentality, and therefore each one of us, finds hardest to understand and to accept. [...] The hardest thing to accept is that it is an event that awakens us to ourselves, to the truth of our life, to our own destiny, to hope, to morality."[146] In this way we can end up seeking refuge and support in something we have thought up and created, something that we deem (albeit implicitly) better suited to attack the nothingness that surrounds us and worms its way into us.

After the initial fascination, why do we fall away and find ourselves in a battle that at times exhausts us? Why

145 Ibid., 49.
146 Ibid., 13.

do we change our method? The choice to set our sights not on the encounter but on what we think we can control better, on what we think will be better able to fulfill us, is strongly, though not in an obviously manifest way, promoted and facilitated by the mentality that surrounds and permeates us. "We are immersed in a 'worldly' reality opposed to what has happened to us. This worldly reality needs the event of Christ, it needs it to be witnessed and lived, but as awareness and affection; it is radically foreign and opposed to the new personality, to the 'new creature' to which Christ gives origin."[147] The contradiction between the newness introduced by the event of Christ and our historical context continually challenges Christians, the baptized. How can we keep from succumbing? Only through the concrete and continual presence of the mystery made flesh who enables us to experience Him through a living Christian reality.

Even though we have been baptized and at a certain point have encountered the companionship of the church, if we find ourselves far from the concrete and continual presence of Christ who engages us through human preference ("Zacchaeus, hurry down from that tree: I'm coming to your home"), we remain alone with our wants, prey to the enticements and strength of those in power, to the images of fulfillment that the context feeds us and that we knowingly or unknowingly make our own.

But the opposite is not a given, either. But be careful: while it is true that without an ongoing bond with the companionship of Christ through the human faces He uses, it is difficult if not impossible not to succumb to the

147 Ibid., 49.

mentality that surrounds us, it is equally true that being immersed in a living Christian companionship does not automatically guarantee that we will not yield to the temptation to substitute for the event encountered something else, to put our hope in something else, to return to imagining a road of fullness based on our own resources. This temptation existed at the beginning, exists now, and will exist for the rest of time, and yielding to it is "sin."

María Zambrano observed this in her original way by looking at the origin: "If we hold to the sacred story of Genesis, [Adam] succumbed to the promising seduction of the future ('You will be like gods') not out of a thirst for happiness, but on the contrary, leaving the happiness that flooded him in order to pursue his own creation, something he had made, and in order not to have to contemplate what was offered him, to flee the pure presence of beings whose name he knew, but not their secret."[148]

Each of us is called to see what happens in our personal and community life when we yield to the temptation to substitute the newness generated by the mystery made flesh with a creation of our own, with something we have made.

2. The temptation to self-affirmation

A look at the history created by the charism given to Fr. Giussani can be very helpful for understanding the factors in play in the Christian journey.

---

[148] Maria Zambrano, *Chiari del bosco* [Clearings in the woods] (Milan: Bruno Mondadori, 2004), 71.

In the years after the student revolts of 1968, in the midst of ongoing pressures from the cultural, social, and political context that to some extent are similar to those we face today, Giussani gave a precise description of this temptation to self-affirmation. This was in 1975, addressing a gathering of adults in the Conservatory Hall in Milan for the usual Beginning Day,[149] but his words are equally pertinent for us today.

Giussani denounced in the reality of the movement a "lessening," a desertification of the experience, a confusion, an anxiety and attributed it to "a lack of method, a lack of attention." How should we understand this lack of method and attention? It lies in the fact that "the foundation, the root of the question, from which everything derives, the source of energy and intelligence, is taken for granted and no longer nourished, no longer cherished and safeguarded, no longer helped by our attention and will, and it tends to disappear slowly and become abstract. In a life like the Christian one, woe to those who take for granted in any way the ongoing origin of our face, of our personality, of our light and of our strength!"[150] In fact, when we take for granted the source, the event that has happened, it changes into an a priori put aside in a drawer; we take the event as a given and then we face reality starting from our own projects and interpretations. The event survives as a category that is well-known and even referred to, but not as the vi-

---

[149] This is the annual gathering of Communion and Liberation members after the summer break, at the beginning of the social year.
[150] Fraternity of Communion and Liberation (hereafter cited in notes as FCL), Audiovisual documentation, *Beginning Day of CL*, Milan, September 14, 1975.

tal root of knowledge and action. Our actions do not start from the Christian event and we do not expect satisfaction, that is, correspondence to the original needs of the heart, from it. Instead, we seek it in our own achievements, in our own capacity for building, in our own affirmation. Through this, without perceiving it, we change method, as noted above.

Giussani identified this lack of method and attention in the "grave prevalence of self-expression, of a search for expression, both personal and collective," in the pursuit of "a naturalistically understood self-expression. We feel an urgent need for the satisfaction of the wants and instinct that fill our personal life and are noted in our collective life. This drive predominates dangerously over the point that constitutes the continual nourishment of our human and Christian journey." In other words, the search for our own self-expression takes precedence over the event that entered into our lives as the origin of a human newness, a new intelligence and affectivity.

What is the root of the problem? Giussani answered without hesitation: self-affirmation as the ultimate goal and horizon of action. "The value we pursue going to church or battling in a factory, school, or university, when we are alone and when we are together, is self-affirmation, according to the aspect that interests us (maybe affectivity, maybe cultural gusto and curiosity, maybe an ability you want to express, maybe social and political passion). The central point is that the value we are pursuing, individually and together, seems to me to be prevalently defined by the need, the presumption, the anxiety to affirm ourselves, according to what interests us, according to what we feel to be interesting for us."[151] It should be noted that Giussani was not talking to people who had chosen to follow other paths, but to those who had chosen the Christian experience he himself had brought forth and who generously invested time and energy into the various spheres of this commitment. This makes his observation even more interesting because it does not concern "others" but "us"; that is, people who are living the Christian proposal that attracted them. In his last book, just recently published, Giussani clarified this sensitive point in terms of an alternative: "Instead of affirming being, reality in its integral and entire truth, in its total, exhaustive destiny, we are determined by the anxiety to affirm ourselves," and went on, "We set our hopes on our own project. This is sin, putting hope in our own project."[152] This is our permanent temptation. Through a strange and deep weakness, and through yielding to presumption, the human person, each one of us, detaches himself from what allows him to live and takes it for granted, which is a way of denying it, and affirms himself. He relies on himself and "fixes his attention and his desire on particular and limited things. The original plan, that for which man is created, was altered by the arbitrary use of freedom. Thus men tend toward a particular, which, when detached from the whole, is identified as life's aim. The experience we live every day is that we tend to identify the totality of life with something partial and limited. Escaping this partiality is not

---

[151] Ibid. "Seek ye first the kingdom and his righteousness, and all these things shall be added unto you. We instead, seek first 'all these things,' and, in a manifest way, do not find them." Tolstoy, *Resurrection*, 306.
[152] Luigi Giussani, *Un avvenimento nella vita dell'uomo* [An event in the life of man] (Milan: Bur, 2020), 187, 27.

in our hands. None of us can, alone, recover a true way of looking at reality."[153]

But the pursuit of self-affirmation does not lead to the fullness and satisfaction it seems to promise; it does not free us from nothingness. Our discourses and efforts are insufficient and sterile attempts at fullness and satisfaction, as we have observed. In fact, all our initiatives "make the dissatisfaction increase disproportionately."[154] The nature of the sin determines its punishment, in what Dante called "the law of counterpenalty," by which "one's punishment reproduces the essential characteristics of the sin." In fact, the "search for self-affirmation in one particular or another that most interests us always results in greater disquietude. This attitude that gives first place to self-affirmation, to the gusto of hearing yourself talk, the gusto of your own self-expression, ruins everything."[155]

Never as in these times of coronavirus have we seen the limits of a certain way of being in reality and how pathetic it is to set our hopes on our own self-expression. As Graham Greene wrote, "Self-expression is a hard and selfish thing. It eats everything, even the

[153] Giussani, Alberto, and Prades, *Generating Traces*, 14.
[154] FCL, Audiovisual documentation. *Beginning Day of CL, Milan, September 14, 1975*. Dostoyevsky wrote in *The Brothers Karamazov*, "Everyone [today] strives to keep his individuality as apart as possible, wishes to secure the greatest possible fullness of life for himself; but meantime all his efforts result not in attaining fullness of life but self-destruction, for instead of self-realisation he ends by arriving at complete solitude." Fyodor Dostoevsky, *The Brothers Karamazov*, trans. Constance Garnett (Digireads.com Publishing, 2019), 268.
[155] FCL, Audiovisual documentation, *Beginning Day of CL*, Milan, September 14, 1975.

self. At the end you find you haven't even got a self to express. I have no interest in anything anymore."[156] In this vein, Giussani noted that "those who are centered on themselves, on their own goodness or intelligence, on the anxiety to be right or the persuasion that they are, end up no longer perceiving reality in its inexhaustible and mysterious otherness. Thus the only enthusiasm they can feel in life is that of being right, of satisfying themselves, certainly not surprise at what happens, at reality that speaks to them, at the grace of being."[157] Being self-centered makes us deaf to reality, its inexhaustible and mysterious otherness, and transforms life into a suffocating bubble.

What we think will give us satisfaction instead leads us into nihilism; giving first place to our own self-expression ruins everything, reduces everything to zero. Why? Because it goes against the law of human fulfillment. "The law of life is what the Lord told us: 'Those who seek themselves lose themselves, and those who accept losing themselves will find themselves. Those who accept losing themselves for Me will find themselves.' This is the concept of conversion."[158]

[156] Graham Greene, *A Burnt-Out Case* (London: Penguin Books, 1960), 46.
[157] Giussani, *Un avvenimento nella vita dell'uomo*, 139. In the same line, de Lubac wrote, "You believe you are illuminated, and you no longer can discern the essential. You no longer know how to discover freshly blossomed around us perhaps the thousand-fold inventions of the Spirit, always equal to themselves and always new." Henri de Lubac, "Le nostre tentazioni nei confronti della Chiesa" [Our temptations regarding the church], in *Meditazione sulla Chiesa*, 200.
[158] FCL, Audiovisual Documentation, *Beginning Day of CL*, Milan, September 14, 1975.

3. Conversion–continually reclaiming faith

Here, therefore, is the alternative indicated by Giussani: "Not expression of self, but conversion of self.
Not public, cultural, or political expression of the
movement, but conversion of the movement. This is
the word! According to His design and timing, God
rewards conversion with His prize in this world–'All
peoples will come to You'–as all the prophets sang for
Israel, on condition that the people remain faithful."[159]

"Conversion" to the event of Christ, not the claim to
your own project, the breathless and harried search for
your own self-expression and self-affirmation, is what
assures us the "prize," the hundredfold here below in
every sense, including our impact on history. But this
is precisely the point where we slip up. Since we often
deem faith and the encounter to be too fragile, and see
them as unable to give us the satisfaction and impact
we desire and to which we aspire, as we imagine it, we
turn our back on the event and set our sights on our
own initiative. Tolstoy captured this attitude and its
consequences: "He thought of himself as a believer, yet
he knew with every fibre of his being that this faith
was emphatically 'not quite right.' And this was why
his eyes were never without sadness."[160]

---

[159] Ibid. De Lubac observes in this regard, "When we can no longer
see in the church that her human merits, when we do not consider
them more as a means, be they as noble as you wish, in sight of a tem-
poral end, when in them we can no longer discover, even remaining
vaguely Christian, first of all a mystery of faith, we will absolutely
cease to understand her." Henri de Lubac, "Il sacramento di Gesù
Cristo" [The sacrament of Jesus Christ], in *Meditazione sulla Chiesa*,
145).
[160] Tolstoy, *Resurrection*, 324.

Now, if God, the meaning of everything, became man and if this event lasts in history and is contemporary in the life of each of us, everything in the life of a person who acknowledges this should revolve around it. "The encounter that marked the start of our journey has the same characteristics. It is definitive and all-embracing; all the details of our life story are part of it." Christ is important to all of life and to all its concrete aspects. "The content of faith–God made man, Jesus Christ who died and is risen–that emerges in an encounter, at a point in history, embraces all its moments and aspects, which are brought as if by a whirlpool into that encounter, and must be faced from its standpoint, according to the love that springs from it, according to the possibility of its usefulness for one's destiny and for the destiny of man it points to."[161]

To highlight that totalizing character, Giussani drew a distinction between "sphere" and "form." "The encounter we have had, which is all-encompassing by its very nature, in time becomes the true shape of every relationship, the true form by which I look at nature, at myself, at others, and at things. When an encounter is all-embracing, it becomes the shape, not only the sphere, of relationships. It not only establishes a companionship as the place where relationships exist but it is the form by which they are conceived of and lived out."[162] This means that the way you look at every detail of reality, every aspect of existence, is shaped by that encounter. You can live everything with unexpected intensity and dignity even when you find yourself

---

[161] Giussani, Alberto, and Prades, *Generating Traces*, 20.
[162] Ibid.

in a situation of constriction. This is not accomplished by "literature"; it is instead lived experience. Etty Hillesum, sitting on a bench in the Westerbork transit camp, wrote, "Here you learn a great deal. For example, that life is far different from how they describe it for you in history books, and that living is a good everywhere, even behind barbed wire and in drafty shacks, as long as you live with the necessary love for others and life."[163]

Deep down, though we almost may not admit it to ourselves, our thought is dominated by skepticism about the impact of the encounter and faith, about the efficacy of the mystery's initiative in the world. The "gentle" method of God, as Benedict XVI called it, seems too gentle to us. "It is part of the mystery of God that He acts so gently, that He only gradually builds up *His* history within the great history of mankind; that He becomes man and so can be overlooked by His contemporaries and by the decisive forces within history; that He suffers and dies, and, having risen again, He chooses to come to mankind only through the faith of the disciples to whom He reveals himself; that He continues to knock gently at the doors of our hearts and slowly opens our eyes if we open our doors to Him. [...] And yet–is not this the truly divine way? Not to overwhelm with external power, but to give freedom, to offer and elicit love."[164]

Because of this skepticism, we prefer (even without saying so, but it shows in how we act) to substitute for

[163] Etty Hillesum, *Lettere* [Letters] (Milan: Adelphi, 2013), 182–83.
[164] Joseph Ratzinger - Benedict XVI, *Jesus of Nazareth: Holy Week. From the Entrance in Jerusalem to the Resurrection* (San Francisco: Ignatius, 2011), 276.

or "help" the event, God's way of revealing Himself and acting, His style, by means of our projects and activity. In doing so, we do not explicitly renounce Christ, but we leave Him in the tabernacle, in the niche of well-consolidated premises. We take for granted the source; we disincarnate it and transform it into an inspiration that justifies what we think and want, our own self-affirmation.[165] For this reason, Giussani invited us to personal and collective conversion.

Conversion! What is it, and why is this the crucial point? "To convert is to continually reclaim faith, and faith is recognition of a fact, a fact that happened, the great event that remains among us. Who had faith two thousand years ago? Those few or many who recognized in that man the presence of something great and supernatural. Something that you did not see in the way you saw Him, but was evidently in Him, because 'Nobody can speak and do the things You say and do, if God is not with You,' as Nicodemus said to Jesus. Therefore, reclaiming faith means continually reclaiming the awareness of and adherence to the mystery that exists among us, the event that exists in and among us: in each of us through baptism, and among us, then, as part of the church of God." If this conversion truly becomes the "project of our life, then we will also be much better equipped to be ready, willing, and able in all the commitments that history will ask of us day by day."[166]

---

[165] Cf. in this regard Congregation for the Doctrine of the Faith, *Letter "Placuit Deo" to the Bishops of the Catholic Church on Some Aspects of Christian Salvation*, 2.
[166] FCL, Audiovisual Documentation, *Beginning Day of CL*, Milan, September 14, 1975.

Giussani continued with more details: continually reclaiming faith means "reclaiming faith as intelligence and as obedience." Thus there are two dimensions of faith, intelligence and obedience, that we must look at carefully.

Let's start with the first. "Intelligence is what perceives the event inside me and you, among us. In fact, faith is a gesture of intelligence," but of an intelligence that is "deeper and greater than the usual intelligence of natural reason, because it penetrates the level of things in which things take on their substance and meaning. Reclaiming faith as intelligence means a continual recognition of the fact that He is among us. 'We who eat of that Bread are one thing only. Each of you are members of the other, and thus each of you carries the burdens of the other.'"[167]

How is it that in today's world, with all its achievements and developments, with all the skepticism and prejudice that rigidify it, we can speak of these things? What authority do we have to do so? Only that of life and experience, or in other words, if a new self-awareness grows in us and with it a new and more human way of being in the situations everyone is living. As Berdyaev said, "Spiritual freedom goes hand in hand not with a passage to abstraction, but to concreteness [...], it is the victory over the power of extraneousness."[168] How can we say, in the words of Giussani, "We are the place where the noble effort of man toward liberation finds its greatest fulfillment"? How can we

[167] Ibid.
[168] Nikolai Berdyaev, *Schiavitù e libertà dell'uomo* [Slavery and freedom in man] (Milan: Bompiani, 2010), 627.

say these things "if the divine reality, the mystery of Christ that is among us and in us is not continually kept present, if it is not the content of a new self-awareness?" This new self-awareness "is truly another way of perceiving ourselves, another way of perceiving the presence of the other, who the other is and what my relationship with him is. 'We are all one thing alone, so that you are members of each other: therefore, you bear each other's burdens.' What are we doing [in the world] if this has not yet become the project of every morning, the project for every day? Our position in front of the world immediately becomes one discourse among many, one ideology among others, and the nth illusion thrown in people's faces."[169]

The second word Giussani used to indicate conversion, the continual reclaiming of faith, is "obedience." So faith is not only intelligence, "the perception of newness within and among us, but also obedience to this perceived and acknowledged reality in and among us, this unity with the mystery of Christ that I am and you are, this unity between me and you. The unity of blood that a mother gives is less deep and definitive than this, as the Lord said as He was walking through the crowd and someone said, 'Master, your mother and brothers are here.' 'Who is my mother and who are my siblings and who are my parents? Those who do the will of the Father, these are my mother, brother, and sister.'"[170]

We will explore this obedience more extensively at the end of our itinerary. Now let's ask ourselves, What

[169] FCL, Audiovisual Documentation, *Beginning Day of CL*, Milan, September 14, 1975.
[170] Ibid.

is the verification that *faith* as *recognition*, as intelligence of the newness in and among us, and as *obedience* to this acknowledged reality, to "our unity in that man, Christ,[171] are real in you and me? What is the verification of conversion? It is a new humanity, a foretaste of the final happiness.

Saint Paul testified to this experience in his letters. "If anyone thinks he can be confident in the flesh, all the more can I. Circumcised on the eighth day, of the race of Israel, of the tribe of Benjamin, a Hebrew of Hebrew parentage, in observance of the law a Pharisee, in zeal I persecuted the church, in righteousness based on the law I was blameless. But whatever gains I had, these I have come to consider a loss because of Christ. More than that, I even consider everything as a loss because of the supreme good of knowing Christ Jesus my Lord. For His sake I have accepted the loss of all things and I consider them so much rubbish, that I may gain Christ and be found in Him, not having any righteousness of my own based on the law but that which comes through faith in Christ, the righteousness from God, depending on faith to know Him and the power of His resurrection and the sharing of His sufferings by being conformed to His death, if somehow I may attain the resurrection from the dead. It is not that I have already taken hold of it or have already attained perfect maturity, but I continue my pursuit in hope that I may possess it, since I have indeed been taken possession of by Christ Jesus. Brothers, I for my part do not consider myself to have taken possession. Just one thing: forget-

---

[171] Luigi Giussani, *Dall'utopia alla presenza (1975-1978)* [From utopia to presence] (Milan: Bur, 2006), 25–26.

ting what lies behind but straining forward to what lies ahead, I continue my pursuit toward the goal, the prize of God's upward calling, in Christ Jesus."[172]

So then, what does it mean to continue the pursuit toward the goal? Does it just refer to the future? In order to clarify the experience underlying this straining forward to what lies ahead, Giussani reflected on the term that Paul and later the Ambrosian liturgy adopted to indicate it. He added an observation that is key for us, for our experience, yours and mine, as people who desire fulfillment. "The prize begins here below. It is the new humanity that was promised. Saint Paul and the liturgy use a very clear term, 'first installment,' which means 'an advance' received here and now toward the final happiness of the future. We are called to experience and live this, and then give it to others, to the world, to people, because this new gift of new humanity is the best council for making sure that people's efforts will not in the end be distorted, distorting, and disappointing."[173]

A new, different, truer, more fulfilled, more desirable humanity is the only "council" that can open a breach in our consciousness as women and men, as contemporary women and men, the only one that can be heard as a fascinating and liberating invitation. These things are necessarily defined on a generic level, but "it holds for your family life, with your wife, your husband, your children; it holds for your work relationships, the relations you must have with every person you encounter,

[172] Phil 3:4–14.
[173] FCL, Audiovisual Documentation, *Beginning Day of CL*, Milan, September 14, 1975.

for every event that happens in good or bad times, so that in good times we are humble and in bad times we are secure, equally."[174]

The conversion of which we spoke leads to this prize, a new humanity, an advance on the final happiness of the future, and is therefore another way of conceiving things, a new knowledge, *a true gaze on reality.*

[174] Ibid.

CHAPTER 5

THE RELATIONSHIP WITH THE FATHER

What is a true gaze on reality? Who has ever had it? Who introduced it into history and who can help us have one?

Jesus lived on this earth like each of us, and as a true man dealt with particular, finite, fleeting things. He endured trials and sufferings, even the extreme suffering of the cross. What enabled Him not to succumb to incompleteness, not to end up in nihilism or desperation in front of the supreme trial? How does Christ help us not be overwhelmed by the incompleteness of things and situations, by the poverty of our attempts at self-affirmation, by the void of meaning, and by desperation?

1. Our life depends on an Other

In *La convenienza umana della fede* (Why faith is humanly worthwhile),[175] Giussani commented on and developed the implications of certain passages of Ratzinger's *Introduction to Christianity*, including this one: "What happens when I myself become a Chris-

---

[175] Luigi Giussani, *La convenienza umana della fede* [Why faith is humanly worthwhile] (Milan: Bur, 2018).

tian, when I enroll myself under the banner of this Christ and thereby accept Him as the authoritative man, as the measure of humanity? What kind of shift in being do I thus accomplish, what attitude to the business of being a man do I adopt? How deep does this process go? What estimate of reality as a whole does it involve?"[176]

Giussani observed that "Ratzinger begins saying that being Christian means submitting yourself to the name of this Christ, 'name' in the Hebrew sense, to this presence, to the power of this presence, 'thereby approving Him,' acknowledging Him, 'as the model man' who must permeate my life, as the criterion, 'the parameter that serves as the norm for all human action'; I should try to act the way He acts."[177]

So then, what is the first change that happens in us, the first newness that is introduced, when we submit to the name of Christ, approving Him as the parameter that serves as the norm for all human action? First of all, "the awareness that our life depends on an other and exists in function of this other! Our life, when we get up in the morning and drink our coffee, when we roll up our sleeves to clean the house, when we go to work, whatever work it may be (there's no difference), our life depends on something other, greater, unavoidably greater, which it exists to serve."[178]

Giussani said that this is the first, fundamental thing that Christ as man, Christ as model of life, as parame-

---

[176] Joseph Ratzinger, *Introduction to Christianity*, 2nd ed. (San Francisco: Ignatius, 2004), 56.
[177] Giussani, *La convenienza umana della fede*, 126–27.
[178] Ibid., 127.

ter, as criterion for action, causes to happen in us: "The awareness that we 'belong to' something greater, that we 'belong to' the Father. You sense this well when you understand that all of Jesus's existence is 'in function of, or serves' the Father. He is the 'property' of the Father; He 'belongs to' the Father."[179] "Father" this is the key word.

In this period, when the coronavirus pandemic has made everyone more aware of our fragility and vulnerability, of our dependence on what happens, the importance of these words is all the more dramatically evident.

The decisive importance of the "Father" was what "the apostle Philip confusedly intuited when, just an hour before Christ was arrested, he asked Him, 'Continue to speak to us of the Father; just for once make us see this Father, and we'll be happy!'" He understood that this word overturned the normal way people view themselves, went to the root of everything and embraced the horizon of everything, because the Father is the horizon of everything, the root of everything, infinitely more than the closest comparison we can make, that of a child just conceived, for whom the total horizon and the total root is the uterus of its mother (mother and father: it is the same)." In fact, it is a matter of an ultimate, radical and continuous paternity. "*Tam pater nemo*, nobody is so much a father. He is the only Father. All our life exists in function of Him, belongs to Him. 'Phillip, have you been with Me so long, and still do not understand? Those who see Me, see the Father.' This is the origin of the tenderness and

[179] Ibid.

bottomless wonder that Dostoyevsky had for Christ, because in the Son, the mystery of the Father, to whom we belong, is made familiar."[180]

To indicate how the mystery–the unfathomable source from whom moment by moment the cosmos and my "I," like the "I" of each person, is born, to whom in the final analysis all being belongs–makes itself familiar, "'Father' is the least distant word we can use: father and mother are the closest symbols, the closest signs of this familiarity. God became one among us, but what Christ as the model of humanity, as the parameter, introduces in us is a deep and ever more permeating awareness that we belong to something greater to whom we can say 'Father.' We must recognize Him in our work and our relationships, to make the former intense and offered, and the latter full of mercy and charity."[181]

What way did the Father choose to introduce us to a deep and familiar relationship with Himself? He sent His Son, making Him a presence that we could perceive, so that through the Son made man by the work of the Holy Spirit,[182] we might "see" the relationship of intimacy to which we are called and the newness this brings to our way of looking at and treating all things.

How did the man Christ enable those who heard and saw Him to become aware of belonging to the Father?

[180] Ibid., 128.
[181] Ibid.
[182] "What He [Jesus] says of the Father and of Himself–the Son–flows from that fullness of the Spirit which is in Him, which fills His heart, pervades His own 'I,' inspires and enlivens His action from the depths." John Paul II, Encyclical Letter *Dominum et Vivificantem*, 21.

Every gesture He offered, everything He said, every gaze of His was filled with, shaped by, and documented His awareness of the Father. "Christ, as a man, was totally determined by this consciousness, such that He could say 'The Father and I are one' (Jn 10:30). If someone were to stop Him as He was walking, talking with the apostles, or eating, and ask 'What fills your consciousness in this moment?' He would have said, 'the Father.' 'I have food to eat of which you do not know. My food is to do the will of the one who sent me and to finish His work' (Jn 4:32–34). Doing His will, this is life." Giussani went on to say that no matter what we do, no matter what journey we are on, "my life is to do His will, not because I am a priest; for me it is exactly the same thing as for you who are a typist!"[183]

We are called to look to this experience of Christ's, to immerse ourselves in it and identify with it, and to compare ourselves against it. If someone were to stop us as we were walking along the street and ask, "What is filling your consciousness in this moment?" what would we say? Clearly, it is not a matter of repeating certain words, but of discovering what actually fills our consciousness as we go about our lives.

What does it mean to be conscious of the Father? Who is the Father? The Father is the origin of all things, the one from whom all things come and proceed, be it a flower in a field or the face of your beloved. What is the connection between Christ's awareness of the Father and His relationship with reality? How does the way He lived His life as a man in relation to the Father interest us?

183 Giussani, *La convenienza umana della fede*, 128–29.

The way of relating to being that corresponds to the heart, that satisfies and does not delude, was made familiar in Christ. We were made for this. "Recognizing reality as deriving from the mystery should be familiar to reason, because precisely in recognizing what is real, just as it is, as God wanted it to be, rather than reduced, flattened out, without depth, we find a correspondence with the needs of our heart, and our innate capacity for reason and affectivity is fully realized. For reason, owing to its own very original dynamic, cannot fulfill itself unless it recognizes that reality is rooted in mystery. Human reason reaches its apex, and so is truly reason, when it recognizes things for what they are, and things as they proceed from an other."[184]

Recognizing that reality comes from the Mystery is not an illusion of dreamers or something of which you have convinced yourself, but the culmination of a true use of reason and affection. How familiar is it to us? How many times have we recognized the mystery when looking at the usual things? It is not a question of being endowed with a special gift. Recognizing reality as the sign of the mystery is within the reach of everyone, as Paul said in his letter to the Romans: "What can be known about God is evident to them because God made it evident to them. Ever since the creation of the world, His invisible attributes of eternal power and divinity have been able to be understood and perceived in what he has made."[185]

However, while it is within the reach of all, it is not taken for granted. On the contrary. Our reason is

---

[184] Giussani, Alberto, and Prades, *Generating Traces*, 14.
[185] Rm 1:19–20.

structurally made to grasp the meaning of reality, but instead, the thing that should be as familiar to reason as it is correspondent to our freedom seems far off in history, out of focus, and we cannot see or grasp it, so much so that when we do recognize reality as a sign of the mystery, we are wonderstruck. This means it is not a habitual experience for us. Perhaps what is habitual for us is another way of relating to reality, one that considers its existence obvious.

What was Jesus's daily experience in relating with people, things, and events, as recounted in the Gospels? Jesus saw all of reality as event. "The dynamic of event describes every instant of life: the flower in the field 'which the Father clothes better than Solomon' is an event; the bird that falls 'and the heavenly Father knows it,' is an event; 'the hairs on your head are numbered'–they are an event. Even heaven and earth, which have existed for a million centuries, are an event: an event that still occurs as something new, since their explanation is inexhaustible. To glimpse something greater in the relationship with everything means that the relationship itself is event."[186]

It is difficult not to be surprised and attracted by Jesus's gaze on reality as described in the Gospels. He shows a way of living reality that does not flatten it out or reduce it; He incarnates and testifies to a true and whole relationship with every aspect of reality. By showing us how He looks at everything from the flower in the field to the bird that falls and the person who suffers, Jesus introduces us to a familiarity with the mystery that is happening now: everything can

---

[186] Giussani, Alberto, and Prades, *Generating Traces*, 12.

be lived as event inasmuch as, in the final analysis, in this moment, it originates from the mystery.

What enabled Him to live reality with this intensity? His relationship with the Father. To put it in the terms used before, Jesus did not set His hopes on self-affirmation or self-expression, but on His relationship with the Father. His miracles were never a display of ability, but always pointed to the Father, and were performed so that people would become aware of the Father and acknowledge that the Father had sent Him. His way of living as a man was not oriented toward self-affirmation, but instead, obedience to the Father's will. His continuous relationship with the Father, which filled his consciousness in every moment, enabled Him to live everything with incomparable intensity and density. In the man Christ we find the full expression of the content of Romano Guardini's line, "In the experience of a great love [...] everything becomes an event within its sphere."[187]

Nothing seized Him like the Father. "The Father and I are one."[188] Not even the evil He suffered separated Him from the Father. Rather, it is precisely there that you see all the density of His relationship with the Father, which led Him to entrust Himself beyond all measure. "This primal trust in the Father, which no mistrust ever clouds, rests on the Holy Spirit common to Father and Son. In the Son, the Spirit keeps alive the unshakable trust that the Father's every ordinance

[187] Romano Guardini, *L'essenza del Cristianesimo* [The essence of Christianity] (Brescia: Morcelliana, 1980), 12. Original German edition, *Das wesen des christentums* (Würzburg: Werkbund-Verlag, 1938).
[188] Jn 10:30.

(even the transformation of the personal separation into abandonment) will always be an ordinance of love, which the Son, now that he is a man, must reciprocate with human obedience."[189] This is the root of the victory of Christ over nothingness. The Son's way of living is the victory over nothingness.

In everything He does, Christ testifies to His relationship with the Father. "Whoever believes in me believes not only in me but in the one who sent me."[190] Everything of His, every gesture or word, points to the Father, to the mystery. Every gaze or action of His is filled with this presence. As Giussani said in a line I've committed to repeating every time I can, "The man Jesus of Nazareth–invested by the mystery of the Word, and therefore assumed into the very nature of God (but His appearance was completely identical to that of all men)–they didn't see this man do one single action whose form didn't show His awareness of the Father."[191] Stressing what characterized the self-awareness of the man Jesus, Giussani drew on the words of John's Gospel: "My food is to do the will of the one who sent me and to finish his work" (Jn 4:34), and "My Father is at work until now, so I am at work" (Jn 5:17). His life was a continual mimesis, a continual imitation, a mirror: His awareness continually mirrored the Father. "I

[189] Hans Urs von Balthasar, *Unless You Become Like This Child*, trans. Erasmo Leiva-Merikakis (San Francisco: Ignatius Press, 1991), 31.
[190] Jn 12:44.
[191] Luigi Giussani, "A New Man," notes from a conversation of Luigi Giussani with a group novices of Memores Domini, Milan, January 31, 1999, *Traces*, no. 3, 1999, available at http://archivio.traces-cl.com/archive/mar99/parola.html

cannot do anything on my own: I judge as I hear" (according to what He hears in His conscience), "and my judgment is just, because I do not seek my own will but the will of the one who sent me"(Jn 5:30).[192]

Jesus lived in the awareness that all of His value depended on His relationship with the Father. Outside this relationship, nothing would have lasted, nothing would have had substance. The Father, the relationship with Him, gave heft and meaning to everything. "We can be sure that the human Child Jesus was in amazement over everything: [...] from the tiniest flower to the boundless skies. But this amazement derives from the much deeper amazement of the eternal Child who, in the absolute Spirit of Love, marvels at Love itself as it permeates and transcends all that is. 'The Father is greater.'"[193]

2. Following Jesus: being daughters and sons

How can this gaze on ourselves and on the world become familiar, in history, for each of us? In the companionship of Jesus. It is worth our while to learn Christ's gaze on reality because "if a man does not look at the world as something given, as an event, starting from the gesture of God which gives it to him now, it loses all its attraction, surprise, and moral appeal; in other words, the appeal to adhere to the order and

---

[192] Giussani, *La convenienza umana della fede*, 129.
[193] Balthasar, *Unless You Become Like This Child*, 45–46.

the destiny of things."[194] Instead, when reality is recognized as event, as originating in the mystery, this produces an incomparable intensity in your own life. "What intensity of life is promised to those who grasp, instant by instant, the relationship of everything with the origin! Each instant enjoys a definitive relationship with the Mystery, and so nothing is lost: this is what we exist for, and this is our happiness."[195]

The relationship with the Father charges every single instant, even the most ephemeral, with meaning, and makes it positive. We need to be aware of this. "There is not one moment / that does not weigh on us with its power / of the centuries; and life in every heartbeat / holds the tremendous measure of the eternal."[196] Otherwise everything crumbles and the void of meaning wins out. For this reason, there is nothing more worthwhile than following Jesus. In following Him, we can claim His promise that those who follow Him will have the hundredfold here below. In the companionship of Jesus, a true relationship with reality can become a stable experience in us. Religiosity, the acknowledged and lived relationship with the mystery that is within everything, which has to do with everything, can become the experience of every moment, and the difference of life that derives from this can become continual. With Christ we lose nothing, because He enables us to enter into a relationship of familiarity with the Father. "After so much conver-

[194] Giussani, Alberto, and Prades, *Generating Traces*, 14.
[195] Ibid., 31.
[196] Ada Negri, "Tempo" [Time], in *Mia giovinezza* [My youth] (Milan: Bur, 2010), 75.

sation and so much time spent in each other's company, we can begin to sense what incredible intensity, nobility, lightness of life, what an incredibly different life this introduces! [...] 'I descended from heaven not to do My will, but the will of Him who sent Me. And the will of Him who sent Me is that I lose nothing of what He gave Me.' That I lose nothing! Jesus referred to the apostles, the disciples, but the meaning can be extended. The will of the Father is that I lose nothing of what He has given me: every moment, every circumstance of life, every provocation, each thing to accomplish. It is a spontaneous intensity, ever more spontaneous, not a fixation."[197]

We see this intensity in one of Bonhoeffer's letters written during his period in prison, which ended with his execution, because of his opposition to the Nazi regime. "For this last week or so these lines have kept on running through my head: 'Let pass, dear brothers, every pain; / What you have missed I'll bring again.' What does this 'I'll bring again' mean? It means that nothing is lost, that everything is taken up in Christ, although it is transformed, made transparent, clear, and free of all selfish desire. Christ restores all this as God originally intended it to be, without the distortion resulting from our sins."[198]

Every circumstance can carry the newness that Christ brought into the world. Our effort does not suffice for this to happen, but this does not mean that our freedom is not needed. Let's look attentively at

---

[197] Giussani, *La convenienza umana della fede*, 129–30.
[198] Dietrich Bonhoeffer, *Letters and Papers from Prison*, trans. Peter Selby, abridged ed. (London: SCM Press, 2001), 40.

what it means to follow Jesus. What is the path that Jesus shows us? Not effort, but being daughters and sons. Jesus teaches us what it means to be children of the Father by showing how He is a son. The life of fullness that He shows is not that of being capable, but of being a son.

Paul reminded the Christians of the young church about the source of this familiarity: "As proof that you are children, God sent the spirit of His Son into our hearts, crying out, 'Abba! Father!'"[199] And again, "You did not receive a spirit of slavery to fall back into fear, but you received a spirit of adoption, through which we cry, 'Abba, Father!'"[200] Benedict XVI commented, "Becoming a human being like us, with His Incarnation, death and Resurrection, Jesus […] accepts us in His humanity and even in His being Son, so that we too may enter into His specific belonging to God. Of course, our being children of God does not have the fullness of Jesus. We must increasingly become so throughout the journey of our Christian existence, developing in the following of Christ and in communion with Him so as to enter ever more intimately into the relationship of love with God the Father which sustains our life. It is this fundamental reality that is –disclosed to us when we open ourselves to the Holy Spirit and He makes us turn to God saying "Abba!"–Father. We have truly preceded creation, entering into adoption with Jesus; united, we are really in God and are His children in a new way, in a new dimension."[201] In fact,

[199] Gal 4:6.
[200] Rom 8:15.
[201] Benedict XVI, *General Audience*, May 23, 2012.

as Schlier noted, in Jesus Christ, being "manifests itself to us, becomes accessible and present to us, becomes our historic experience in 'being in the Spirit' [...]. In fact, in the Spirit, Jesus Christ manifests Himself and yields Himself to experience."[202]

This becoming daughters and sons is explored beautifully by Isaac of Stella in his *Sermons*. "Could a servant of God seek anything greater than to become a son of God? Why brothers, we could not even dare dream of such a privilege did not God's kindness permit and promise it to us."[203] A bit further on, Isaac states that "the Word Omnipotent [...] declared: 'This, Father, is my desire, that as we are one, these may be one in us' (Jn 17:11). How loving the divine desire, worthy of god, full of gracious charity, a truly valid assurance of Truth! 'That as we are one, these may be one in us.' What heights for a slave to reach, what forgiveness for an enemy! From enemy to slave, slave to friend, friend to son, son to heir, from heir to one spirit or even one thing with the inheritance itself! You would have to annihilate him to deprive him of this inheritance itself! You would have to annihilate him to deprive him of this inheritance that is none other than God himself."[204]

Our mistake is to think that Jesus is different because of His superior capacity, which enables Him to do what

---

[202] Heinrich Schlier, *Linee fondamentali di una teologia paolina* [Fundamental streams of a Pauline theology] (Brescia: Queriniana, 2008), 156.

[203] Isaac of Stella, *Sermon Five: A Fifth Sermon for the Feast of All Saints*, in *The Selected Works of Isaac of Stella: A Cistercian Voice from the Twelfth Century*, trans. Daniel Deme (Routledge, 2017), 24.

[204] Ibid., 28.

we cannot; that is, to live without yielding to nothingness. Instead, Jesus does not diminish or become arid, is not the victim of nothingness, because He lives for the Father. This is His one strength: "I have life because of the Father."[205] He is different not because He is more capable of being Himself autonomously, but because He is a Son. This is the full qualitative difference of Christ.

The content of His self-awareness is the relationship with the Father. "'The one who talks about himself seeks his own glory' [self-affirmation], and this cuts our head off: just think of when we argue. 'But the one who seeks the glory of Him who sent him, this one is truthful.' He does not seek the affirmation of his own points of view, but the affirmation of truth full of attempt and of humility, in the search for the 'opinion' of Him who sent us."[206]

What does it mean not to seek affirmation of our own points of view? It is a different conception of the conscience. "The word 'conscience' as used by Christians means the total opposite of the word as used by modern people. Modern people use it ('I follow my conscience') to mean the place where you generate your opinions and thoughts; they have the right to affirm what they think and feel because they understand themselves as the source of everything. Conscience is conceived of as the source of criteria and opinions." Instead, for Christians, the conscience is "the place of self where you seek and listen to the truth of an other. Therefore, Christians are by nature humble, and when the thing

205 Jn 6:57.
206 Giussani, *La convenienza umana della fede*, 130.

is clear, they are very certain, humbly certain, and fully prepared to put their energies into action for a quest to 'hear,' as the Gospel of John first said: 'But the one who sent me is true, and what I heard from Him I tell the world.' We say what we have heard."[207]

Is it strange or arduous to listen to the truth of an other and speak about what you have heard from an other? No, Giussani responded, referring to the adults to whom he was speaking. "You do it all the time. I take that back: you do it often." You just need to become aware of it. "How great it is to be aware of doing it, catching yourself as you tell your children things or encourage them to do something, or as you tell your friends things, because it is the same, catching yourself speaking to your children and being able to say, 'He who enables me to speak this way is truthful, and I say the things I heard from Him; I'm telling my child the things I heard from Him.'"[208] When this new consciousness is in action in your relationship with your children, "what tranquility, what security, what peace there is! You are also free from your child's response. Instead, when it's your opinion that matters, you want the child to accept it at all costs, and you try to dominate."[209] These are very concrete signs of a verification of whether the new consciousness generated by Christ has begun to penetrate our innermost being.

Thus the important thing is that the consciousness of the Father become increasingly familiar so that each person can say, like Jesus, "The one who sent me is with

[207] Ibid., 130–31.
[208] Ibid., 131.
[209] Ibid.

me." This experience matures over time as we continue the journey, never ceasing to travel the road that the encounter continually opens up before us, as we said. "Just think of a person who ten, a hundred, a thousand times a day is conscious of the fact that He who sent him, He who makes him, the mystery who makes him, is with him, that God is with him: this is the reason for the serenity you see on the faces of certain monks and nuns, and also for the striking serenity that you see on the faces of many of our friends, because these things live among us."[210]

These moments of awareness can shape every instant, every gesture, every gaze, our way of facing everything, step by step. "'I come from God; I don't come from myself!' I'm not saying it to you; I'm saying it to myself," Giussani emphasized, as he reminded his listeners that "each of you should say it to yourselves. I don't come from myself; I come from an other and therefore I must do the works of Him from whom I come. I need to listen, look, and imitate. If at some moment in His life a person approached that youth or that man, Jesus of Nazareth, and asked, 'What are you thinking about?' Jesus would have said 'the Father,' but not abstracted from things." In fact, thinking of the Father and thinking about or taking care of things are not separate. "Thinking about the Father is a true way of thinking about things. It is *the* true way of thinking about things. It is a way of looking at things that you bring to your wife or husband, to your children, to your work, to the good or the bad things that happen to you, to yourself."[211]

[210] Ibid., 132.
[211] Ibid.

Jesus reveals the mystery to us as Father. He is the one who taught us to say "Our Father." So, perceiving moment by moment that everything is related to the origin means perceiving that everything is related to the Father, and this makes us see all things in their truth, entirety, and usefulness. "Do you think that the relationship with the mystery, with the Father, as Jesus taught us, and thus the imitation of Christ, keeps you from looking at your man or your woman, your children, or flowers and things? No, it enables you to look at them in a way that is a hundred times more intense and true. Thus even stutteringly, we comprehend that truth lies here; even through our stuttering, we perceive that the truth comes to us from here."[212]

3. Sin is forgetfulness

The relationship with the Father does not take us away from things or suppress them, but fills them with meaning. Thinking of the Father is the true way of thinking about things. This is a gaze that is finally true, and everything takes on a unique density and intensity. Finally you affirm the value of the moment, of relationships, work, reality, and circumstances and sufferings, your own and those of others.

The signs of this true way of treating everything are freedom, peace, imperturbable certainty, trust, and abandonment. ("Into Your hands I commend My spirit.") Anxiety no longer wins out in us; we are no longer determined by the success of our self-expression, no longer dominated by fear and uncertainty. "Why torment ourselves when it is so easy to obey?" says Anna Vercors in Claudel's *The Tidings Brought to Mary*.[213]

And yet, there is so much deceit and unfairness in how we think about and treat ourselves, others, and things! We often ask ourselves where this comes from, and right away say that it is due to sin, but without really knowing what sin truly is. We immediately think of our failures of energy, strength of will, and coherence. This is the symptom of a tendency to moralism that overshadows what we live and renders so many of our days opaque.

So then, let's try to look at sin more deeply without veering off into moralism. The experience of sin is "literally the faltering of this awareness of the Father, or in other words, the faltering of the striving to have this awareness happen." In fact, "if I am bound to this 'greater than me' […] and if my nature is to live consciously, then if I abandon the consciousness of this relationship, this is sin! Sin is human action that abandons the consciousness of this relationship. […] True sin, the substance of sin is this forgetfulness. So you see how important morning and evening prayers are! How important it is to pray the Our Father! You should slow down and pray it attentively, reflecting on the words, so that at least for one moment out of twenty-four hours you become human, because then it influences everything!"[214]

---

[213] Paul Claudel, *The Tidings Brought to Mary: A Mystery* (Charleston, SC: BiblioBazaar), 95.
[214] Giussani, *La convenienza umana della fede*, 134.

The true problem is not primarily a lack of energy, strength of will, or coherence, but forgetfulness,
forgetfulness of familiarity with the Father. It is not
a problem of capability. When we are not conscious
of the Father, that is, conscious of being children, the
scope of living is reduced. It becomes pure affirmation of ourselves. We do everything "for an ephemeral goal, and this throws everything into nothingness.
If we act only for ourselves, we throw everything into
nothingness. Ninety percent, or rather, all of our actions have this terrible destiny and we have to make
a journey to counter it." Therefore, when there is no
growth in our consciousness that our life is in function of something greater, and this awareness "does
not underlie everything we do," over time "we throw
everything into nothingness."[215]

Acting for ourselves means throwing everything into
nothingness; everything becomes ephemeral because it
lacks depth and meaning. Our actions, the things we
have to do, lack an adequate goal. Life is reduced to ap-
pearances and flattens out: eating, drinking, family life,
work, free time, etc. In the end there is nothing worth
living for, nothing that can attract us and make things
meaningful. In fact, the value of things depends on the
meaning they have and the intensity of consciousness
with which we live them.

Giussani recounted a meaningful episode that happened during his early years as a teacher. "I remember,
and I told my students about it during the early years
when I taught religion, that soon after the war, when
trains still had livestock cars, I was in first class, re-

[215] Ibid., p. 135.

turning from a trip to San Remo for Caritas of Milan (directed by Monsignor Bicchierai), but even in first class we were very crowded. Close to me was a very distinguished older man, maybe about seventy years old. He said he had gone to San Remo to make a very big donation to a convent, and then added, 'Look, I (and he didn't tell me his name) have achieved everything I wanted in life, and I have tens of buildings and factories (he was a big industrialist) but here I am at the age of seventy, and I wonder if I have lost my life.'"[216]

How can we today learn that familiarity with the mystery, with the Father, and therefore our relationship with reality, that Jesus brought into history? It holds the possibility of not succumbing to the temptation of nihilism, to the suspicion that there is no substance to reality or to ourselves, to the doubt that life is positive. What can generate children like Jesus today?

---

[216] Ibid., 135–36.

CHAPTER 6

CHILDREN IN THE SON

We have seen that Christ's consciousness was dominated by his thoughts of the Father, was defined by the awareness of the Father. So if we follow Christ, if we decide to follow Him, "the consciousness of God must penetrate what we do, and slowly over time it will become habitual. […] The thought of God is closely connected to everything, or in other words, it coincides with a way of seeing everything, your wife and yourself, your good and your sin, such that your good does not become pride and your sin does not become desperation."[217]

At this point a question can arise. Jesus taught the disciples the awareness of His relationship with the Father. "To those who did accept Him He gave power to become children of God."[218] Who teaches us about it today? Christ is always the one who introduces us to the relationship with the Father. How does He do this?

1. Through the company of believers–the charism

As we have said above,[219] Christ breaks into my life today and draws me to Himself through a presence, a precise

---

[217] Giussani, *La convenienza umana della fede*, 133–34.
[218] Jn 1:12.
[219] See here, pp. 61-70.

and specific flesh, a persuasive encounter, through which I can have the same experience of relationship with Him as the first people who encountered Him. Through the Son, in the relationship with Christ present here and now, we become children and learn to say "Father," learn to recognize as "Father" the mystery who makes us. The term Jesus used, "Abba," expresses a previously inconceivable and unthinkable familiarity with God.

As it was two thousand years ago, we become "children in the Son" through faith and baptism, in which we receive the Holy Spirit, the Spirit of Christ, "the precious and necessary gift that makes us children of God"[220] and members of the body of Christ, the church, the "people brought into unity from the unity of the Father, the Son and the Holy Spirit," according to Saint Cyprian's beautiful description quoted in *Lumen Gentium* 4, enriched by "hierarchical and charismatic gifts" given so that we can contribute in various ways to building it up and to its mission. The letter *Iuvenescit Ecclesia* on the relationship between the hierarchical and charismatic gifts refers to the principle of the "coessentiality" of these gifts articulated by John Paul II; it quotes Pope Benedict XVI's affirmation that "in the Church the essential institutions are also charismatic and indeed the charisms must, in one way or another, be institutionalized to have coherency and continuity. Hence, both dimensions originate from the same Holy Spirit for the same Body of Christ, and together they concur to make present the mystery and the salvific work of Christ in the world."[221]

---

[220] Benedict XVI, *General Audience*, May 23, 2012.
[221] Congregation for the Doctrine of the Faith, *Letter "Iuvenescit Ecclesia"*, 10.

For this reason, the movements and new communities formed through the Spirit's gift of charisms testify to how the church does not grow "through proselytism but 'through attraction.'"[222]

Pope Francis never fails to remind us of these new realities about openness to mission, the need to obey pastors, and ecclesial immanence, since "it is within the community that the gifts the Father showers upon us bloom and flourish; and it is in the bosom of the community that one learns to recognize them as a sign of his love for all His children."[223]

We belong to God the Father; we are "His" in the deepest sense of the word, that is, we are His creatures. "But our creaturely dependence would remain an enigmatic and fleeting perception if it had not been revealed clearly in Christ [in His Spirit]: 'For no-one has seen God: the only-begotten Son who is in the bosom of the Father, has made Him known.' In belonging to the God who has become Man" and entered into history, "our total [and ultimate] dependence, our 'being made' becomes clear."[224] The belonging is to Christ, "not to our idea of Christ, but to the real Christ, the one who remains in history within the unity of the believers who are united to the pope, the bishop of Rome."[225]

Today the Son makes the mystery of the Father familiar to us through the church and becomes event for us through the grace of the encounter with a charism;

---

[222] Francis, *Evangelii Gaudium*, in Congregation for the Doctrine of the Faith, *Letter "Iuvenescit Ecclesia*," 2.
[223] Congregation for the Doctrine of the Faith, *Letter "Iuvenescit Ecclesia*," 10.
[224] Giussani, Alberto, and Prades, *Generating Traces*, 50.
[225] Giussani, *La verità nasce dalla carne*, 54.

in our case, the charism given to Fr. Giussani. The Spirit of God, in His infinite freedom and imagination, can "bring into being a thousand charisms, a thousand ways for man to partake in Christ. A charism is precisely the mode of time, of space, of character, of temperament, and the psychological, affective, intellectual way with which the Lord becomes event for me, and for others in this same way. This way is communicated from me to others, so that between me and *these* people there is an affinity that is not there with everyone else; a stronger, more specific bond of fraternity. This is how Christ remains present amongst us every day, till the end of the world, within the historical circumstances that the Mystery of the Father establishes, and through which He has us acknowledge and love His presence."[226]

Thus the charism is "evidence of the Event present today, inasmuch as it moves us. [...] If the charism is the mode with which the Spirit of Christ makes us perceive His exceptional Presence, then it gives us the

---

[226] Giussani, Alberto, and Prades, *Generating Traces*, 79. In *Letter "Iuvenescit Ecclesia"* we read, "The charismatic gifts are given to individual persons, and can even be shared by others in such ways as to continue in time a precious and effective heritage, serving as a source of a particular spiritual affinity among persons." (John Paul II, Apostolic Exhortation *Christifideles laici*, n. 24: *AAS* 81 (1989), 434). The relationship between the personal character of the charism and the possibility of sharing it expresses a decisive element in its dynamic, insofar as it touches upon the relationship that, in the ecclesial communion, always links person and community (Cf. ibid., n. 29: *AAS* 81 (1989), 443–46). The charismatic gifts, when exercised, can generate affinities, closeness, and spiritual relationships. Through these the charismatic patrimony, originating in the person of the founder, is shared in and deepened, thereby giving life to true spiritual families. The new ecclesial groups, in their diverse forms present themselves as shared charismatic gifts." *Letter "Iuvenescit Ecclesia,"* 16.

power to adhere to it with simplicity and affection."[227] The charism brings the church alive and exists in function of all of ecclesiastical life. "Each of the historical modes with which the Spirit puts men in relationship with the Event of Christ is always a 'particular,' a particular mode of time and space, of temperament, of character. But it is a particular that renders one capable of the whole."[228]

John Paul II acutely observed that "the charism's own originality, which gives life to a movement, neither claims nor could claim to add anything to the richness of the *depositum fidei*, safeguarded by the Church with passionate fidelity. Nonetheless, it represents a powerful support, a moving and convincing reminder to live the Christian experience fully, with intelligence and creativity. Therein lies the basis for finding adequate responses to the challenges and needs of ever changing times and historical circumstances. In this light, the charisms recognized by the Church are ways to deepen one's knowledge of Christ and to give oneself more generously to Him, while rooting oneself more and more deeply in communion with the entire Christian people."[229]

This dynamic is represented well in the following testimony. "I joined the Fraternity of CL this year, at the age of fifty-nine, when people normally finish things, not begin them. I'll start by saying that I'd been around the movement a lifetime because of a swarm of cous-

---

[227] Giussani, Alberto, and Prades, *Generating Traces*, 80.
[228] Ibid., p. 80.
[229] John Paul II, *Message to the World Congress of Ecclesial Movements and New Communities*, Rome, May 27, 1998.

ins, and through them Fr. Giussani's message reached me sideways, so to speak. The thing that fascinated me was finding the answer to the question, Who am I? Am I Christian at home, having lunch with my family, and then at school am I nobody? Am I a believer at Sunday Mass, and then at the film club am I something else? How could I fit together what I felt inside, not like educational baggage, but as a need, with everything that I encountered outside, the uniform post-1968 thinking, the superficiality of a preconceived judgment? It was a continual question, a search in every sphere, to find the unifying factor that would make sense of that puzzle. An initial orientation to that question and a concrete possibility came in Fr. Giussani's invitation to 'live reality.' Obviously, it was common sense, and I'd seen it in my grandparents, who didn't divide their faith and their life. Their every gesture was steeped in faith, naturally; it was second nature for them. Instead, in my daily life I found myself questioning everything–and everything became illogical. I felt disorientation, division, and superficiality in my relationships, in not touching keys that should be made to play. But I had heard, almost overheard, a teacher who indicated a path for me, a solution, and with that little crumb I carried on: 'live reality.' An intense life, four children, a lot of work, many difficulties and many successes, a full, coherent life, one of continual searching, because all that hustling and 'doing' was a search, a desire; it was stumbling around blindly, trying different roads, all the roads possible. I begged for a confirmation, for support as soon as possible, but I didn't find it. I found applause for my coherence or remonstrance for my exuberance; judgments, but not communion. Then an unexpected event happened when someone pinned me down and asked, 'Do you have a living Christ inside?' Not an answer: a question. And the answer was already there, in front of me: it had His face, a living Christ inside me, today, here beside me, not a Christ that will be there only at the end, but already here, now, at this moment, for me. That moment changed my life and then my way of praying. I don't accumulate points anymore in the tiresome effort to follow preestablished frameworks. Now I experience closeness, listening, expectancy, and abandonment. My way of moving in reality has changed into 'living' reality with a presence alongside me, and therefore with a different gaze, the same gaze that I experienced upon myself, the gaze that changes the person in front of you because you are the one who has changed. All the things I'd read and tried to learn, to study, to understand in my life were something else: not toil, but evidence. And this evidence, if pursued more deeply in a companionship, is the music for my soul that I had always been searching for."

If the companionship generated by the charism in the church and for the church strikes and attracts us, it is precisely because "it makes the encounter with this Man a concrete experience. It takes away the abstraction and makes us experience it as a reality that we can live today. The companionship is not an idea, a discourse, a logic, but a fact, a presence that implies a relationship of belonging."[230]

[230] Giussani, Alberto, and Prades, *Generating Traces*, 50.

2. Authority: a present paternity

Thus the concrete companionship where the encounter with Christ happens becomes "the place of belonging of our self, from which it draws the ultimate way of perceiving and feeling things, the way of grasping them intellectually and of judging them, the way of imagining, planning, deciding, and doing. Our self belongs to this 'body,' which is the Christian companionship, and from this it draws the ultimate criterion for tackling everything. Only this companionship, therefore, enables us to face reality, makes us touch reality and makes us real."[231]

So then, let's ask ourselves now, with Giussani, "What is the most important factor in the reality of people to which we are called, in the reality of the companionship in which we participate?" In answer, he said, "The most important factor in the reality of a people is called *authority*."[232] Authority is the most important factor of the reality of a people because without it, a people is not generated. Authority is the place where it becomes evident that Christ is victor, where Christ persuasively shows that He corresponds to the needs of the heart. "Authority is a person who, when you see him or her, you see that what Christ says corresponds to your heart. By this a people is guided."[233]

[231] Ibid.
[232] Luigi Giussani, "La gioia, la letizia e l'audacia: Nessuno genera, se non è generato" [Joy, gladness and audacity: No one generates unless he is generated], *Tracce-Litterae communionis*, no. 6 (June 1997): II.
[233] From a conversation between Luigi Giussani and a group of Memores Domini, Milan, September 29, 1991, in "Chi è costui? [Who is this man?], suppl. to *Tracce-Litterae communionis* 22 no. 9 (October 2019): 10.

In our society, the word "authority" is often viewed with suspicion, identified with power that subjugates or with a cult of personalism that binds people to oneself. But Giussani stressed that in the life of the church, in the people of God, this cannot be the case. "Authority, the guide, is precisely the opposite of power; there is not even a smidgen of the word power. For this reason, fear is completely absent in front of the concept of authority in the people of God, at every level, because fear corresponds to power, and to free yourself from fear you have to not give a fig about power."[234]

So then, what characterizes the relationship with authority, the belonging to the people of God? This relationship is well expressed by the word sonship, according to Péguy's distinction between being disciples and being daughters and sons.[235] Belonging implies the relationship between a daughter or son and a parent, not that between a student and a teacher, and does not involve rote repetition. Through filiation, the accent of a true companionship, the originality of a charism, of "that form of teaching to which we

---

[234] Ibid.

[235] Péguy wrote: "When the student does nothing but repeat not the same resonance, but a poor repetition of the master's thought; when the student is no more than a student, even though he be the best of all, he will never generate anything. A student does not begin to create unless he introduces a new resonance (in other words, unless he is no longer a student). Not that he should not have a master, but one must descend from the other by the natural ways of fathering, not by the scholastic ways of discipleship." Charles Péguy, *Cahiers* VIII, XI, [February 3.1907].

have been entrusted,"[236] enters into us. Giussani reminded us that everyone is a child of authority. "A son receives his family tree from his father. He makes it his own; he is made up of that family tree his father gives him, he is made up of his father. Therefore, he is entirely absorbed. Authority absorbs all of me. It is not a word I fear or dread or that I follow. It absorbs me. The word, 'authority,' then …the word 'authority' could have as its synonym the word 'paternity,' meaning generativity, generation, the communication of a genus, communicating a living family tree. That living family tree is my "I," which is overtaken and made different by this relationship. The word 'authority,' which coincides with the word 'paternity,' is followed by the word 'freedom.' It generates freedom. Being a son or daughter is freedom."[237]

Authority is a present paternity. In order to be "children in the Son," in order to be children in Christ, not in the Christ in our mind but in the real Christ present here and now, and therefore in order to be introduced into a relationship with the Father, you have to live a present paternity: it is necessary that there be a presence that generates us as children. Giussani said, "Having a father is a permanent attitude because it belongs to your history [to the story of each person given

---

[236] This is a well-known expression of Ratzinger: "Faith is an obedience of heart to that form of teaching to which we have been entrusted." Joseph Ratzinger, *Intervento di presentazione del Catechismo della Chiesa Cattolica* [Intervention at the presentation of the catechism of the Catholic Church], in *L'Osservatore Romano*, January 20, 1993, p. 5. Cf. Rm 6:17.

[237] Luigi Giussani, "Joy, Happiness and Boldness: No One Generates, Unless He is Generated," *Journey, The CL Magazine*, no. 2, 1997, p. 11.

that everyone has had a father. But here is the crucial point...]. If in 1954 I had not entered the Berchet, but another school, my life would have been altogether different. Your attitude is permanent, but generation–the interesting part of paternity–is presence, something in the present."[238]

There is no flowering of our personality, no true creativity, without filiation, without the experience of being generated. "No one generates, unless he is being generated. Not 'unless he has been generated,' but 'unless he *is being* generated.' This concept of paternity is the one most attacked by the whole Enlightenment culture,"[239] and very often, even among Christians, among us, who have had the grace to run up against the charism given to Fr. Giussani, through which we have been able to discover in a new and vibrant way what we are talking about here.

"You can't be a father, a generator, if you have no one as your father. Not [pay attention here] if you *didn't have*, but if you *don't have* [in the present] someone as your father. Because if you have no one as father, it means there is no event, it is not an encounter, not a generation. Generation is an action in the present."[240]

Jesus introduces us to His familiarity with the Father by calling us to live a present paternity in the companionship to which He attracted us. Through this paternity, Jesus's relationship with the Father becomes ours, yours, and mine. In order for this new-

[238] Ibid.
[239] Ibid.
[240] Ibid.

ness to happen, in order for the relationship with the Father to totally permeate our life so that it becomes the parameter of all our thoughts and actions, even the most ordinary and banal, a paternity *now* is necessary, that is, it is necessary to be generated *now* by a presence in which Christ becomes an evident and persuasive reality that can be experienced. You can be children in the Son only if you are being generated now. Without this generation in the present, a relationship with the Father cannot become consciousness and life in us, and no effort will have the power to save us from nothingness.

Giussani underlined in an incomparable way the essential need for this "now." "The 'event' does not indicate only something that happened and with which it all started, but what awakens the present, defines the present, gives content to the present, and makes possible the present. What we know or what we have becomes experience if what we know or have is something that is given to us now–there is a hand that offers it to us now, there is a face that comes forward now, there is blood that flows now, there is a resurrection that happens now. Nothing exists outside this 'now'! Our 'I' cannot be moved, aroused, that is, changed, if not by something contemporaneous–an event. Christ is something that is happening to me. Now, in order for what we know–Christ, the whole question of Christ–to be an experience, there has to be a present that provokes us and arouses us. It is a presence as it was a presence for Andrew and John. Christianity, Christ, is exactly what He was for Andrew and John when they followed Him. Imagine when He turned around, how they were struck! And when they went home with Him… It has been just like this up to now, up to this moment!"[241]

However, it is not enough that this paternity be present: I must be willing to let myself be generated by it. The fecundity of our life depends on our willingness to be daughters and sons. "It is what Jesus said to Nicodemus: 'You must be born again.' 'How? Born again? Do I have to enter my mother's womb again to be born again?' 'Those who are not born again do not understand the truth of reality, the truth of things.' This understanding is a rebirth."[242] Those who agree to follow Him, becoming daughters and sons, will be surprised by the newness that begins to happen in their lives.

3. Obedience

Giussani encouraged us to take a further step that he deemed crucial for the growth of a new self-awareness. We said above that conversion is the recovery of *faith* as *recognition*, as intelligence of the newness in and among us, and as *obedience*. We promised to return to this word.

"The obedience to which this intelligence invites us has inevitably, as it were, a kind of *passum sub iugum* to be endured, to be taken into consideration: you have to deal with what we call 'authority.' What I am going to remind you of holds both for the authority of

---

[241] Luigi Giussani, text of the 2011 Easter Poster of Communion and Liberation, https://english.clonline.org/pubblications/posters#pretty-Photo[obj11255]/9/.

[242] Giussani, *La convenienza umana della fede*, 130

the church made by Christ, the bishop united with the others and with the pope, and by analogy to inferior, though real and pedagogically crucial levels, for any presence of the factor 'authority' or 'authoritativeness,' in the Christian life."[243]

It is necessary to pay attention to this point, because "without this sign"–authority–"there would be no companionship among us, no ministry of the church, no new people of God journeying in the world, for the good of the world: without authority there would not be the newness that Christ called us to live together."[244]

In speaking about the journey of conversion in 1975, Giussani observed that "the factor of authoritativeness or authority is pedagogically crucial: if we neglect this factor we become dust that the least little breeze picks up and scatters all over the face of the earth; we return to being like children, as Saint Paul says in the second chapter of his letter to the Colossians, 'tossed by the waves and swept along by every wind of teaching arising from human trickery, from their cunning in the interests of deceitful scheming.'" Therefore, Giussani continued, "authority among us is not a cultural opinion to be discussed; it is not the offer of an opinion like any other. The function of authority is a proposal in which the unity of our entire human and Christian experience is at stake."[245]

In the following passage, he underlined the nature of authority and of the relationship to which it consequently calls each of us. "Authority, inasmuch as it proposes an

[243] FCL, Audiovisual Documentation, *Beginning Day of CL,* Milan, September 14, 1975.

[244] Giussani, *Un avvenimento nella vita dell'uomo*, 229.

[245] FCL, Audiovisual Documentation, *Beginning Day of CL*, Milan, September 14, 1975.

experience of life, even in particular details, asks us to engage our entire person. Authority is the supreme sign of
the mystery, of the mystery of the Father's design. It is the
supreme sign of the mystery that is among us as history
that is in process, becoming, developing." Since authority
is the supreme sign of the mystery among us, "the attentive devotion to the authoritative function is obedience,
out of obedience to the Lord, not out of desire to win an
argument. Thus in front of it, there is the exercise of faith.
For this reason, there can be no authority among us unless it is within true faithfulness to the unity of the entire
movement. Analogously, the movement would have no
authority if it did not seek intensely to live this devotion
to the authority established by Christ."[246]

This passage also offers us signs and criteria for
recognizing and evaluating all authority within the
Christian companionship in which we are involved.
Giussani gave a very precise description: "What we say
in the movement is always pedagogical, with the goal of
reaching a more mature understanding of the church
in our life: [the movement] is the experience the Lord
has called us to live in order to reach that goal. For
this reason, a position of authority that does not assert
itself and is not felt and perceived within a deep faithfulness to the life of the entire movement, to the unity
of the movement, does not hold, is not followed. Or, if
it manages to be followed it is despotic and alienating,
coming out of despotism and the will to command in
some way. Authority in the worldly sense is a stumbling block, and not constructive."[247]

---

[246] Ibid.
[247] Ibid.

Authentic authority is an essential factor for constructing anything, while authority in the worldly sense, as power, is alienating despotism, a stumbling block, and not constructive. But these observations go beyond the sphere of Christian experience, and have to do with a need and a dimension that concerns everyone, believers and nonbelievers alike. What happens in Christianity is an intensification and concretization of the human dynamic. So then, beyond specific figures, authentic authority (*auctoritas,* i.e., that which causes to grow) is an indispensable factor for the growth of the "I," for the construction of our personality. In our life, we experience authority as an encounter with a person with a rich consciousness of reality who introduces us to the complex of circumstances, incarnating a hypothesis of meaning for adequately interpreting and facing them, calling us at the same time to put it to the test, to verify its substance personally. Thus Giussani went so far as to state that "in a certain sense, authority is my truest 'I.' But today it frequently happens that an authority is perceived as something external that is 'added on' to the individual. The authority remains external to the person's mind, even if the person may devotedly accept the authority as a limit."[248]

When this external aspect prevails, authority is perceived as an obstacle to the growth of the "I" and not as a factor for its maturation. In virtue of this extraneousness that is both promoted and lived, Giussani observed, "Today's culture holds that it is impossible to know and change yourself and reality 'only' by following a person. In our era, the person is not seen as the

[248] Giussani, *The Risk of Education,* 42.

instrument of knowledge and change, because knowledge and change are understood reductively, the first as an analytical and theoretical reflection and the second as praxis and the application of rules. Instead, for John and Andrew, the first two who happened upon Jesus, it was precisely by following that exceptional person that they learned to know in a different way and to change themselves and reality. From the moment of that first encounter, the method began to unfold in time."[249]

Albert Camus, in his intense autobiographical novel, *The First Man,* provided us with a testimony about the constitutive need for an authority that is not added externally to one's "I," but is instead paternity. "I tried to find out for myself, from the start, when I was a child, what was right and what was wrong–because no one around me could tell me. And now that everything is leaving me I realize I need someone to show me the way […] by right not of power but of authority, I need my father."[250]

This is what is realized in the Christian experience, showing itself in all its essential nature. "In order to build, you need solid, absolutely firm ground, otherwise you are unable to build. What solid and firm thing do we need, if not the mystery of Christ who is among us and of whom we are certain through the immanence of His church, through obedience to the authority of this church, which has cost us so much and will cost us even more?"[251]

[249] Luigi Giussani, "Dalla fede il metodo" [From faith the method], in *Dalla fede il metodo*, 18.
[250] Albert Camus, *The First Man*, trans. David Hapgood (New York: Alfred Knopf, 1995), 34.
[251] FCL, Audiovisual Documentation, *Beginning Day of CL*, Milan, September 14, 1975.

After these words about obedience, Giussani returned to the initial point of his reflection, warning his listeners against creating an antithesis between the search for your own satisfaction and the search for your own conversion. Remember, he was speaking in 1975, but his words are fully pertinent to our situation. "So I would like all of you to reflect very well on this antithesis, which I believe poses the danger of a separation: on the one hand, between the root that nourishes, the source that nourishes our intelligence of faith, our will, our energy for Christian engagement, and on the other hand, the activity that is asked of us by the historical circumstances in which the Good Lord has caused us to live. Unfortunately, it has befallen us to live in a time when you can't sit back in your armchair because the house is burning. The human house is burning. Well. In this antithesis I see a danger that favors the disassociation of the root from the flower of the plant; the plant detached from the root is destined to dry out. In this antithesis, your presence in the movement, in the community, in the Christian life as such, is either a search for your own satisfaction or instead a search for your own conversion."[252]

The radical nature and clarity of this antithesis promotes and in some ways makes inevitable a comparison with ourselves. The danger, a temptation for each of us, is to slide into "the search for self-affirmation according to what you think, feel, and are interested in, instead of changing these criteria. It is no coincidence that the first word for the Lord was "*metanoia*": you have to change the criteria of evaluation. The value of

[252] Ibid.

life, and thus the value of the movement, of the community, the value of our engagement in CL, does not lie in how much it satisfies interests that are important for you (because it brings you esteem, gives you friendships or a girlfriend or a boyfriend, or enables you to have your ideas accepted): the value lies in the conversion to faith that happens [in you]. Therefore, let's focus on this."[253]

4. "The hundredfold here below"

For us and for others, the easiest way to be prompted to conversion is through the testimonies of life that reach us. Allow me to offer two among the many that, by grace, surround us.

Before the coronavirus pandemic broke out, I received this letter that offers a simple example of the ongoing conversion of which we are speaking.

"Last year was pretty hard. My husband and I were totally immersed in our new jobs and after a while we realized that we were losing each other: we were just surviving, to the point of having serious difficulties in our relationship. We had little time for anything, very few friends, and those few lived very far away. At a certain point we had to stop and ask ourselves what had been lost. We decided to take a step back in our respective careers and to start doing School of Community again,[254] after having neglected it for months. In order

253 Ibid.
254 She is referring to the permanent catechesis of the movement of Communion and Liberation.

to do so, we had to hire a babysitter, an added cost to that of daytime childcare, and decided to commit our one free evening to spend together. We found right away that in going to School of Community together we were happier. It was evident, and it was something that also helped our relationship. I was surprised by the welcome we received, which I never would have imagined, and every week I'm amazed by the new arrivals. The way many speak about their encounter with Christ in every moment of their journey and the questions they ask provide me the opportunity to encounter anew the same presence that won me over in the beginning. It's happening anew for me! After fifteen years in the movement I've never felt so happy to go to School of Community. We try to do this work during the week too, and it illuminates our days. School of Community teaches me another way to look at reality, one that is more true and whole. Since we began to follow again, we find we are more open with people we meet because we want to recognize in everyone the reverberation of His presence and to live the same fullness of heart. The way Christ has entered into my life, through a gaze full of compassion and fondness for my person, is the one thing that truly corresponds to my real desire. All the rest comes later. And we have realized that we can catch the reverberation everywhere, thanks to the renewal of the first encounter. Now it has many faces! It's exciting to see His companionship in our neighbors, in our parish priest, in our colleagues, and in the little things that help us simply by happening. The work that we have done this year in following has been precious: we have recognized what truly sustains us with a more mature, conscious, adult, free, and joyful faith. Thank you for having helped us to make this journey of discovery and awareness. 'Without Me you can do nothing,' Jesus said at the Last Supper. Our experience has shown us that this is true."

As Saint Bernard wrote, "What comes to us from God, we cannot conserve or keep without Him."[255] In other words, unless His presence happens again and we follow it, we cannot reproduce those fruits we have savored. The journey to truth is an experience: herein lies the full genius of Fr. Giussani's educative method.

I would like to propose a second testimony, significant because of the newness of life it documents. It was written by a young woman who is unable to have children. "Four years ago I got married and my husband and I began right away to try to conceive a child, but it still has not arrived. There have been very difficult times when crying was the order of the day and nobody, from my husband to my friends, could calm me. For me, everything depended on this child who didn't arrive. I identified the totality of my life with something partial, as if my one chance at happiness was the fulfilment of my desire for maternity. At a certain point my husband said, 'Listen, let's go talk to the priest who married us.' Knowing that the first thing he would ask was whether I had been faithful to School of Community, I got a head start and began reading the text so I wouldn't have to say no. We were reading *Why the Church?* and at a certain point I read, 'The Church's function in history, then, is that of the mother calling back her children to the reality of

[255] Saint Bernard, *Sermone I, 1*, in *Sermoni sul salmo 90* [Sermons on Psalm 90], ed. Monaci Benedettini di Praglia (Bresseo di Teolo (PD): Edizioni Scritti Monastici, 1998), 7–8.

things: man's dependence on God, a merciful God. [...] If we live the consciousness of our original dependence [...] then all problems will fall within a framework which will make solving them easier. [...]And because this method of looking, in fact, would be focused on Something larger than the individual problem, it would confer on everything the prospect of a constructive path to pursue."[256]   Lungfuls of clean, fresh air! I was surrounded, above all, by my husband and friends. One day a friend called and, speaking about herself, said, 'You get pregnant, you're happy, but then you realize that not even this is enough. The point is what grounds our life.' Immediately and inexplicably, I stopped crying, from one day to the next. I am the one who changed. I'm serene and I can tell you this story without crying. I changed, not because of definitions, but through faces and facts. I found myself on a journey and with a new gaze on my difficulties, which have not gone away, but now I have a gladness not of myself that enables me to entrust myself completely to the design of an other and that ultimately fills me with gratitude. The difficulty remains, but I can look at it serenely. Augustine said, 'My heart is restless until it rests in Thee.' In order for me to loosen my grip on what I have in my mind, an other must fill my life. I can't take away the desire, that's there, but now I can let go of the demand that the answer come the way I think it should. I'm waiting expectantly for an other to fulfill my desire; I'm attentive to perceiving this response. Starting again from Christ, the difficulty is no longer a crushing weight. But as soon as I shift away from Christ, the anxiety and fear move in and my

[256] Giussani, *Why the Church*, 152–54.

thoughts and crying take over again. Instead, when I start from His presence, the ultimate judgment is this underlying gladness and peace that fill my life. Looking at my whole life, I know that Christ will not cheat me. When I decide to start again from Christ, His presence makes my life more true, human, and beautiful. This is a miracle to me and to the others."

How can we not remain in silence, full of wonder, in front of such a testimony of humanity changed by an encounter with the carnal presence of Christ? Giussani's words help us perceive its full import. "Christ did not come to say, 'Those who follow Me will find satisfaction for all their whims and in their thoughts and interests.' No! He said, 'Those who follow Me must change their criteria, begin to transform their criteria for evaluation, valuing, and the judgment of value.' And, if you do this, you will have the hundredfold even of what it seemed you lost. 'Those who follow Me will have eternal life and the hundredfold here below.' No proposal in the world is clearer and sharper than this one because it challenges us in experience. 'Those who follow Me will be more, will find more, one hundred times more.'"[257]

Those who choose to follow Him, to be a child in the Son, become a new subject, "a new protagonist on the scene of the world,"[258] as Fr. Giussani said at the Synod of Bishops on the Laity in 1987.

[257] FCL, Audiovisual Documentation, *Beginning Day of CL*, Milan, September 14, 1975.
[258] Luigi Giussani, *From Baptism, a New Creature*, address of Fr. Luigi Giussani at the Synod of Bishops, Rome, October 9, 1987. https://english.clonline.org/archive/fr-giussani/from-baptism-a-new-creature

This newness is our mission in the world. "The meaning of our personal and collective presence in the world, our capacity to encounter women and men, our capacity for encounter, is founded only on a newness, a newness of life that lies in experience today. Only to the extent to which we experience today a relationship with Christ and a new relationship among us through His presence, only to the extent to which we have this experience today, will we be able to create new humanity around us and more peace among the people around us."[259]

5. "For the world, love alone is credible"

I would like to conclude with Giussani's wish for those listening to him in Milan in 1975 so that each of us may cherish it in our hearts as a support for the daily journey ahead of us. "We will always be up to our necks in moral, physical, personal, and social troubles, but we will never collapse, as Saint Paul says in his Second Letter to the Corinthians, chapter four, verses 7–10: 'We hold this treasure in earthen vessels, that the surpassing power may be of God and not from us. We are afflicted in every way, but not constrained; perplexed, but not driven to despair; persecuted, but not abandoned; struck down, but not destroyed; always carrying in the body the dying of Jesus, so that the life of Jesus may also be manifested in our body,' and therefore, in this world."[260]

[259] FCL, Audiovisual Documentation, *Beginning Day of CL*, Milan, September 14, 1975.
[260] Ibid.

If we are faithful to the grace that has reached us through the charism of Fr. Giussani,–we who were attracted by this charism and desire to follow it–if we live the movement as personal conversion to the present event, "centered in Christ and in the Gospel," we can be "the arms, hands, feet, mind, and heart of a church 'which goes forth,'"[261] collaborating with the pope for the future of the church in the world, a future described by Cardinal Ratzinger on the long-ago Christmas of 1969:

"The future of the Church can and will issue from those whose roots are deep and who live from the pure fullness of their faith. It will not issue from those who accommodate themselves merely to the passing moment or from those who merely criticize others and assume that they are infallible measuring rods. [...] To put this more positively: the future of the Church, once again as always, will be reshaped by saints. [...] From the crisis of today the Church of tomorrow will emerge–a Church that has lost much. She will become small and will have to start afresh more or less from the beginning. She will no longer be able to inhabit many of the edifices she built in prosperity. As the number of her adherents diminishes, so will she lose many of her social privileges. In contrast to an earlier age, she will be seen much more as a voluntary society, entered only by free decision. As a small society, she will make much bigger demands on the initiative of her individual members. [...] In faith and prayer she will again recognize the sacraments as the worship

---

261 Francis, *Address to the Communion and Liberation Movement*, Saint Peter's Square, March 7, 2015.

of God and not as a subject for liturgical scholarship. […] One may predict that all of this will take time. The process will be long and wearisome […]. But when the trial of this sifting is past, a great power will flow from a more spiritualized and simplified Church. Men in a totally planned world will find themselves unspeakably lonely. If they have completely lost sight of God, they will feel the whole horror of their poverty. Then they will discover the little flock of believers as something wholly new. They will discover it as a hope that is meant for them, an answer for which they have always been searching in secret. And so it seems certain to me that the Church is facing very hard times. […] She will enjoy a fresh blossoming and be seen as man's home, where he will find life and hope beyond death."[262]

Echoing this prophecy about the new perspective opening in this time, Fr. Giussani said, fewer than fifteen years later, "This is a moment when it would be beautiful to be just twelve in the whole world."[263] He did not say this to be presumptuous or exclusive, but because he was aware that we have come full circle, as it were, to the beginning of everything. And, as in the beginning, the one thing that can save us from nothingness is the experience of a newness of life today.

Only this newness can be credible today. "The Christian grain of wheat possesses a genuine formative fruitfulness only if it does not encapsulate itself within a particular form set alongside all the forms of the

[262] Joseph Ratzinger, *Faith and the Future* (San Francisco: Ignatius, 2009), 116–18.
[263] Luigi Giussani, *Certi di alcune grandi cose (1979-1981)* [Certain of a few great things] (Milan: Bur, 2007), 396.

world, an illusory form that thus condemns itself to sterility, but following the example of Jesus, squanders itself and offers itself up as a particular form–without being afraid of the dread of being abandoned and of letting go of oneself. Indeed, for the world, love alone is credible."[264]

[264] Hans Urs von Balthasar, *Love Alone is Credible*, trans. D. C. Schindler (San Francisco: Ignatius, 2004).

Table of contents

CPSIA information can be obtained
at www.ICGtesting.com
Printed in the USA
LVHW020606230920
666822LV00004B/392